From Queendom To Kingdom

The "Call," The "Charge," The" Mandate"
The Memoirs of a Rising Trafficking Queen Pin

Dr. Marie Baker

Copyright © 2023 by Dr. Marie Baker

This book or any part of this book may not be taught or reproduced in any form, without prior written permission of the author except as provided in the United States of America copyright law. All rights reserved. Unless otherwise indicated, scripture quotations are from the New King James Version (KJV) Copyright © 1982 by Thomas Nelson. Used by permission.

Copyright © 2023 by Dr. Marie Baker
All rights reserved.

Special discounts are available on bulk quantity purchases by book clubs, associations, and special interest groups.
For details, email: QueenBBaker@gmail.com or call 706-386-4698.

ISBN: 9798387975424
Printed in the United States of America
First Paperback Edition

VERY SPECIAL

DEDICATION

This Book is Dedicated to My Late, Loving, God-Yahweh Filled and Led Mother: Mrs. Tommie Scott Baker, whom the Lord called home on November 29th, 2018, at the graceful age of 95. She taught me everything I know today; from cooking, cleaning, praying and so much more. I dedicate this book to you for loving me, for teaching me everything that you knew and setting the foundation.

Rest Well, in Power and Peace. Enjoy Heaven.

To My Father, My Daddy: Mr. Sheppard Baker for truly I was my "Daddy's Little Girl", my "Daddy's Baby".
I Love and Miss! You. Rest. On

VERY SPECIAL ACKNOWLEDGEMENTS

I start this page with special acknowledgements to some of the people that were instrumental, in not just helping me to prepare this amazing book. When this book is read, you will realize the influence that their lives and words had upon my life.

To the Late Great Mother-Prophetess Corine Manuel; although you are at a peaceful rest, I thank you and your trusted friend, Mother-Apostle Bettye White for allowing God to use you to activate and cultivate every gift that was locked up on the inside of me; and bringing them to the surface. Thank you for the prophetic words that were spoken that changed the very course and direction of my life. God used you both in so many ways to jump start and shape the "Kingdom Leader That I Am Today". "Thank You"! Rest Well and Enjoy Heaven.

To Apostle Dr. Vanessia M. Livingston, of Miracle Deliverance Prophetic Temple of God; for being that Mother in Zion and Spiritual Midwife that was sent to me. Not only did you coached me, you also groomed, nurtured, and mentored me; thank you for teaching me how to properly walk in the office of my chosen call. Thank you for your truths. Thank you, for teaching me how to love again, especially how to properly love God's people. God has used you in so many ways to shape the Kingdom Leader That I Am Today. Thank You! Kingdom Blessings. NO FEAR!

To the Late Great Dr. Mother Gertrude Stacks, my heart is broken as I reflect upon the last time that was shared and the words that you spoke into and over my life while wrapped in your loving and caring arms in Savannah Georgia in 2019; every towel wrap, every shot, every charge; I came with the spirit of expectation, I wanted more! I vow to fulfill the Call, the Mandate and the Predestined Assignment as Promised. Rest Well and Enjoy Heaven.

To the Late Minister Jerolene Moore-Wilburn (Flood), you wore many hats in my life in so many ways. Thank You for the push, support with Judah Dove, in ministry, and your prayers and intercession. God used you in many ways to shape me into the Kingdom Leader I Am Today. "Thank You Very Much!" I promise to fulfill your request as you laid on your bed of death. I vow to fulfill every word! Rest Well and Enjoy Heaven.

To Mother Judy Hines, for an experience that changed the

way that I thought about life, prayer, and ministry. It gave me a greater understanding and insight. It birthed out greater and stronger levels of prayer, fasting, and denial of people, places, and things; as well as total submission that was needed in my life and the works that were ahead. God has used you in several ways to mold me into the Kingdom Leader I Am Today. "Thank You Very Much!" And Kingdom Blessings.

To Bishop Dianne R. Collins, Thank you for your love and support. Thank you for opening your heart, sharing your ministry, and your time. Thank you for Covering Me, PMB Ministries and Judah Dove LLC-The Dove Love Center. God has used you in several ways to mold and shape me into the Kingdom Leader I Am Today. "Thank You So Very Much!" And Kingdom Blessings.

Dr. Percy Johnson, a Bible Scholar, in his own rights. I thank you from the bottom of my heart for teaching me how to rightfully divide the "Word of God" and to recognize truth when I hear it. "Ye shall know the truth, and the truth shall set you free," says the Bible (John 8:32 KJV). Thank you for being so firm in your stance to make me to dig. It was my boot camp of study that led to my being an honor student. God has used you in so many ways to shape the Kingdom Leader I Am Today. "Thank You!" And Kingdom Blessings.

To Dr. Caroline Driver, let me begin by saying that encountering you during my search for significance definitely turned the light on. The words you spoke and released into my life; they have all been instrumental in my becoming the "Change Agent" That I Am for Many Others. It Is Here, and the Books-Workbooks will follow (Self-Worth). Thank You! And Kingdom Blessings.

Table of Contents

VERY SPECIAL DEDICATION..3

VERY SPECIAL ACKNOWLEDGEMENTS..4

INTRODUCTION 9

CHAPTER 1   THE "CALL OF THE CHOSEN".....................................12

CHAPTER 2 "THE CHARGE" FIGHTING FROM A "SECRET PLACE"
....39

CHAPTER 3 "THE MANDATE" 63

CONCLUSION..140

ABOUT DR. MARIE BAKER..149

INTRODUCTION

Let me begin by mentioning that this book has been in the works for more than twenty years. But God-Yahweh's timing was an important factor to consider, especially while carrying out His will in my life. God will tell us what He will do for us, but we must wait for Him to do it.

I was told by many people, some of whom are named in the acknowledgements of this book, that there will be books to come from me, some of whom are not listed because there were many. During those years, the devil threw everything but the kitchen sink at me in order to divert and postpone God's prophecy. But I believe that each attack has made me stronger. The difficulties, tribulations, emotions, setbacks, and set ups all had an emotional, relational, and spiritual impact on me. But it was the love of God-Yahweh that kept me (Ps. 139-24 NIV) "Search me, O God, and know my heart; test me and know my anxious thoughts. See if there is any offensive way in me and lead me in the way everlasting".

As a proud mother of three, grandmother of four amazing grandchildren, and established woman in ministry, and holder of several degrees, including an Associate of Arts in Counseling, a Dual Bachelor of Arts in Biblical Theology and Criminal Justice, a Dual Master of Arts in Leadership, and a Master of Divinity. In addition to being a recipient of a doctrinal in Humanitarianism, I am a 501 C3 holder with a background in public safety in law enforcement as a "Deputy Sheriff", "Class President and Top of My Graduating Class", Correctional-Detention Officer, Fire Fighter-EMT, Educator within the Educational-School System, Life Coaching, and Entrepreneur. I was predestined from birth to lead in the world and the kingdom.

My Greatest Achievement, I believe, was the day Jesus Christ came into my life and I accepted Him as my Lord and Personal Savior. He was and remains to be my Life, Strength, Joy, Comforter, and Healer, among other things. Every course and season of my life contributed to my arrival at this place and time in GOD. This Book is being released at the Perfect Time! "Gods Timing is Everything".

To everyone reading this book, we have problems, deep emotions, and spiritual scars from neglect, abuse, manipulation, verbal, and perhaps physical abuse; and for some, sexual abuse; and for many, church abuse. However, we must apply God's Solution, which includes the Word of Truth, deep or deeper prayer, and great or greater consecration. You must be willing to go and be taken to another level-realm in the spirit.

Every season of your life is a course, a class, and you will be graded with a "Pass" or a "Failure", determining whether you must repeat the course. My prayer is that the Lord will bless, heal, deliver, and set you free from whatever strongholds you may be experiencing; that you will pass every course, every test and trial.

I pray that this book will help someone in their quest for freedom from past and present unhealed hurts, unresolved issues, wounds, and scars, as well as how God wants to reveal His Presence in your life through your kingdom assignment.

CHAPTER 1

THE "CALL OF THE CHOSEN"

Life was very simple and basic for me, with simply the necessities to live and survive. Born as the eighth and last child to a strong and staunch woman of God, one could hear prayers and calling on the name of Jesus in the early hours of the morning; one that would get up early to prepare breakfast for her family while singing and humming old hymns. I recall my mother making a lot of my garments, but they were gorgeous because the queen made sure I was always covered; to me, she could transform a Crocker sack into something lovely.

She always tried to make sure that we had what we needed for church and school. We didn't always receive nor have everything we wanted or needed, but mom always found a way. But her greatest and most distinctive quality was her love for God-Yahweh. God, The Lord was always first and foremost in my mother's life. My mother was and still is a model of what a Christian-Saint should look like. Proverbs 31:10 says "Who can find a virtuous woman, for her price is far above rubies? (KJV) That verse, I believe, was speaking of my mother.

I recall getting dressed and being taken to church, sometimes two or three services a Sunday. Church was never an option in my mother's house, and you had to be ready when she was. The most important rule in the house was that everyone goes to church. "Joshua 24:15" Says as "For me and my house we will serve the Lord". I was told that as a baby with my mother and a bottle in my hand, I would be in the choir stand trying to sing with the choir, from Baptist, Pentecostal, and Apostolic churches. "Remembering what the Bible in Proverbs 22:6 King James Version Says (KJV) "Train up a child in the way he should go: and when he is old, he will not depart from it". I clearly found this to be true as I ran, but I couldn't hide.

Listen, it is God that calls, and chooses you. The Bible says that Jesus is the head of the Church (Colossians 1:18), and it is He Himself who chooses who should enter full-time ministry (Ephesians 4:10-11). No one should enter ministry on a whim or just on a desire to do good, or for financial gain. If you are not called, you will not have the grace or the gifting to do it; as a result, you will be frustrated, the life of God will not be in it, and it will be just a job, without satisfaction.

People who are called to ministry are called supernaturally. They are people who will serve; people who will have a stronger desire for God and His things than the average Christian. Is God calling you to ministry? If so, prepare to die to yourself while also preparing for the most magnificent journey in faith, blessing, satisfaction, and power you will ever have in your life. You have been given a magnificent gift, but it is now time to prepare for it.

As I continue, having the opportunity to raise children is a true blessing. This applies to both believers in Christ and those who do not have a relationship with God. However, if you are a believer, it is important to leave a spiritual legacy for your children to pass on to their children. I learned to pray at my mother's knees, and whenever she prayed, I would be on my knees beside her. At a young age, my mother taught me "The Our Father Prayer," as I called it, I grew up loving and depending on my parents for everything.

My mother placed a high value on prayer. Prayer time with my mother was another time of teaching for me as a child. She taught us to thank God and pray before meals (thanking God for our daily provisions).

She also taught us on a regular basis to believe that there is a God who wants to talk with us and build a relationship with us. This became increasingly important as we grew older; with some reaching adulthood and deciding that it was critical for them to continue believing and trusting in God.

When we raise our children, they must see us continuously putting Christ first in everything we do, including how we spend our time (on Sundays, put Christ first, not sports or travel plans) and how we spend our money (teach and show your kids that you give to the local ministry of the church). My mother taught us to give (tithe) in church by givingus money to put in the Sunday offering. It is your responsibility as parents to teach your children the Bible and about God. Sure, the church can help, but don't overlook your responsibilities to teach your children about God. The church is also a tremendous resource for this, but it must begin with us as parents. To raise children as parents you must "tap into the mind and wisdom of God".

I remember several Sundays when my two older sisters and I had to sing on church programs. Some Sundays, we went from church to church, returning home occasionally for a late-night snack before retiring to bed; from this, I learned and was taught to prioritize God and family. Every day of the week, we went to church; there were "Baptist Training Union" meetings, choir rehearsals, revivals, leadership meetings, and other activities.

Our relationship with God comes first, followed by our commitment to our family; our family should be a priority. This may appear to be a simple, but Christians frequently struggle with it. We get so caught up in trying to love others that we sometimes neglect our own families. If we want to have a healthy connection with God, we must all recognize that our families must be priority; this will lead to a deep prayer and consecration relationship. Your children will be able to tell whether or not they are a priority. I never felt less prioritized with my mom; my mother's first ministry was to pray for her family at home.

My sisters and I progressed from singing Baker Children to Baker Girls and Baker Singers. We were always in church for Baptist Training Union, chorus rehearsal, prayer, and other activities. Don't get me wrong about church there were times when you couldn't wait to get there because you knew there would be food!

Yes, everything you could think of would be on the Church's tables, sometimes it takes the form of a large picnic with everything taking place outside.

Collard greens, mustard greens, turnips, black eyed peas, and string beans would be fresh and prepared the old-fashioned style, full of meat and well-seasoned. There would be pans and pans of macaroni and cheese, dressing, potato salad, coleslaw, and I can't even begin to tell you how many homemade cakes and pies would be made from scratch and with love; anyone hungry yet? I am. These were known as "Family Day"and "Homecoming Services," and dinner was served after the service.

I recall the deacons or elders with the large tubs mixing and making Kool aide and fresh lemon aide with lots of lemons, sugar, and ice, and you could drink as much as you wanted till it was all gone. I always made sure I was close by when it was almost empty so I could collect some lemons from one, if not both tubs, which was the nicest part; I was a very active child who was constantly racing and running around.

My mother not only took us to church, but she also made sure we were members of a church.

(Genesis 18:19) For I have chosen him, that he may command his children and his household after him to keep the way of the LORD by doing righteousness and justice, so that the LORD may bring to Abraham what he has promised him." Let me state that you and your children must be connected to a church. Being connected with fellow Christians is in our life's blood as Christians. This is especially important for your children because they will most likely have other friends outside of church who were not raised in a Godly manner and can be negative influences in their lives. Other Christian children are not perfect, but they often have a much better value system than those who do not attend church. Some parents believe that dropping their children off at church and going about their business is adequate. This sends a negative message to your children, which they will quickly recognize. If it is not important enough for you to stay, your children will believe it is not important enough for them to stay. (2 Corinthians 6:4) KJV "And ye fathers stir not your children to wrath: but bring them up in the nurture and admonition of the Lord".

As a child, I recall spending time alone with my dolls, as any little girl would, but my mother would always question, "Who are you talking to?" because she would always hear me talking as if I were talking to someone. I told her it was a friend of mine, the Lord. "I knew you before I made you in your mother's womb," says Jeremiah (1:5, 31:3). "Yes, I have loved you with an everlasting love; therefore, with loving-kindness have I drawn you".

When I didn't have a playmate, I talked to the Lord Jesus Christ and the angels like I would any other human being. I recall my mother teaching me the "Our Father Prayer", as I called it; as well as how to forgive and love people. She taught me to invite the Lord into my heart. I heard my mother surrender all her children to the Lord and affirm Him to be The Lord-God over us.

My mother was and yet remains my rock; she took me everywhere she went. If I was not around, she would call out for me. I learned how to cook, and I mean cook; from baking cakes, pies, and biscuits; all from scratch. I cooked, prepared my first meal at eight years of age. The meal consisted of fried chicken, field peas with snaps, rice, gravy, homemade biscuits; and ice-cold Kool-aide. My favorite was Red.

She taught me how to put love in everything you cook by taking my time and making it right and to never rush. My mother taught me how to mend things by hand with a needle and thread; and of course, she taught me how to clean.

As I grew older, I began to have and pay close attention to my dreams and visions, which I clearly did not understand. I had to realize that most dreams come from God and are an inaccurate reflection of our individual situation; they are, none the less, symbolic.

As a child, I had a vision of myself going on a walk, which I did frequently, and discovering a bag containing money. I didn't think much of it until it happened: I discovered this bag and opened it to find a beer can containing what appeared to be a large sum of money. Anything more than five or ten dollars was a lot of money when I was a kid; it was the change from a one-hundred-dollar bill from the beer purchase. The receipt was stashed in the bag. As I grew older, my visions and dreams became even clearer, seeing things and having them all come true just as I envisioned or dreamed them.

According to Job 33:14-16, 29, "For God speaketh once, yea twice, yet man perceiveth it not. In a dream, in a vision of the night, when deep sleep falleth upon men, in slumbering upon the bed; then He openeth the ears of men, and sealeth their instruction... Lo, all these things worketh God oftentimes with man".

I was too young to understand them as "hidden wisdom" from God. Something special was hidden within me; dreams were the most common method God spoke with individuals in the Bible. Dreams in the Bible may appear bizarre or ludicrous, but their interpretations are extremely reasonable. The Bible teaches that in the past, God communicated with saints and sinners alike through dreams, warning, directing, and assisting people. He continues to do so. By carefully studying the Bible to discover how God communicated with men in the past, we cannow learn His method of communicating with us.

As I grew older, I saw that people began to frequently tell me that I was someone special in and to God. They would go on to say that God would use me greatly. I was too young to understand what they were saying, and to be honest, I didn't want to hear or understand what they were saying; all I wanted to know was where it was all coming from. I did not know that *Acts Chapter 2:17 says "And it shall come to pass in the last days, saith God, I will pour out of My Spirit upon all flesh: and your sonsand your daughters shall prophesy, and young men shall see visions and old men shall dream dreams".* When I went to other churches, I was told that "The Lord speaks to you." I had no idea what that meant as a young girl, and to be honest, I didn't want to know. All I knew was that I believed in God, which was enough for me. I knew I wanted to be left alone and have fun like everyone else. I didn't care how they knew what they knew; I simply wanted them to leave me alone. But this is where my journey began.

As a child, I did not have the same privileges as other children to do things and visit places that other children did, but I did have a lot of love and care from my mother and father. I was the youngest of eight children, yep, the baby. I was frequently told that I was spoiled and that my mother allowed me get away with everything, which meant that if you did something wrong, you would almost surely be disciplined by her.

When it came to you doing something you knew you weren't supposed to do, my mother, as I now say, did not play the radio. She was a disciplinarian; you were punished based on where you acted up or out. She would just offer you one warning, which was a simple look.

My mother had this look that she could and did give that would warn you that you were treading on thin ice. Please understand that I saw my mother get the older siblings, and it was enough for me to know that what my mother was giving out was nothing I wanted to be a part of. I laugh today as my elder sister said what my mother issued back then would be considered child abuse today, but trust me, there was one or two of them who deserved what they recieved; you know, the kind who just wouldn't listen. *Proverbs 13:24 King James Version (KJV): "He that spareth his rod hateth his son: but he that loveth him chastened him be times"*.

Let me say that it would take another book written to entertain you; yes, if you know me, and trust me, you'd be on the floor laughing. Maybe one day I'll gain permission from my brother to publish the story of the Safari Men. Okay, let me move on before I am tempted to say a few lines to you.

I appeared to be a happy child even though we didn't have much, but I had a secret that I carried around like dead weight. It was so heavy that I was afraid it might kill my mother as well as my father. My secret was that I had been molested by someone close to me, and like most victims-survivors, I was told never to tell anyone. It was said to be our little secret. I was a child, and I knew no better than to keep the secret because I had never been taught to inform someone if I was inappropriately touched.

In this day and time, parents should teach their children that "you're the boss of your body" and that body's safety is important; this can be taught in simple ways that children can grasp. It is typically easier for parents to discuss the differences between right and wrong with their children, but it is often more difficult for parents to discuss sexual development with their children. Children begin to explore their bodies at a very young age by touching, poking, pulling, and rubbing different body parts, including their genitals. As children get older, they'll need guidance learning about these body parts and their functions.

This is something that must and should be done, so please make time as a parent and grandparent to have that conversation.

Parents should use methods to help their child or children in revealing areas where they have been inappropriately touched. Please do not force any kind of touch; always use proper words when describing body parts. Please keep the right tone in mind when addressing this with them—showing concern and love. Discuss the difference between good and bad touch; use simple rules and scripts to assist them in gaining a clear understanding. Please continue to assure them that they may and should come to you if they have been made to feel uncomfortable in any way. There must be openness and trust; they must feel comfortable sharing with you.

Parents need to know when a child's sexual conduct looks to be more than harmless curiosity. Sexual behavior problems can endanger your child's and other children's safety and well-being, and they can indicate physical or sexual abuse or exposure to sexual activity. Finally, if your child is uncomfortable around certain people, please pay close attention and believe them when they tell you something. Children are not born liars; rather, they are taught and trained to lie.

Remember that unwanted phone call or call from a bill collector when your parents said to you, "Tell them I'm not home," and you response to the caller was "My momma says she not home?" I know you're in tears laughing because this happened to you, or you can relate in some manner. But that is the start of educating a child on how to lie and not speak the truth to parents or anyone else. So, now that I've let the cat out of the bag, and to answer your question, no, I never revealed my secret to anyone as a child.

Let me say this: whenever there is a call of the chosen, Satan is out and about, looking for someone to devour: *1 Peter 5:8 "Be alert and sober-minded; be alert, for your adversary, the devil, prowls around like a roaring lion, seeking whom he may devour."* Please take the time to read the book of Job thoroughly; yes, that wonderful book will open your eyes, increase your faith, and assist you in making a total and humble commitment to God. I'm talking about an intimate connection! Simplify your life by making a life decision and committing to it.

My family was not as privileged as others. My older brothers had to work to get the things they wanted and to help with household bills. But, as time passed, I got more interested in things I enjoyed and began to do some of the things I wanted. I became involved in sports and other school activities. I went on school trips for out-of-town games, choral events, and other activities. I continued however to experience dreams and visions, as well as encounters with people, some of whom I felt were extremely religious, and some of whom I found myself running and hiding from at times.

There were times when I would be at the park with friends and would see a certain individual named Joanne Marshall-Brunson. I would hide behind cars, sometimes jumping into the back seats and floors of cars; while telling my friends to shield me from her view. Everywhere that she saw me, she would have a word from the Lord, a word that I was chosen, that God was going to use me in ministry. I did not know, and I especially did not care to hear what she was saying; the truth be told I could not see this, due to all that I had experienced and wanted to do myself. Hear me now!

I had no desire to hear these things because all I could think about was living a better life and making up for what I lacked. I wanted the things I saw my friends with. The nice clothes, shoes, and experience they would share and discuss. I felt terribly deprived. If God had blessed them, then why hadn't he blessed me? But what I did not know was the words that were being spoken would change the course of my life.

I was running away from the person, but I had no idea I was running away from God. But believe me when I say, you can run, but you can never hide from God. The Lord's eyes are everywhere. I didn't want to hear what I already knew to be true. I was aware that something was going on with me. There are two significant days in your life: the day you were born and the day you discover why.

I never thought it strange that I could dream of something, and it would come to pass weeks or even days later. When I looked at someone, it was as if I could see right through them. I simply didn't understand, and I wasn't trying to understand at the time; I just wanted to be normal and have fun like any other young person. But I was not normal, just as God is not normal or common.

He is all-knowing in the sense that he is aware of your past, present, and future. Nothing takes him by surprise. His knowledge is total. He knows all that there is to know and all that can be known.

So, if you are reading this book and believe that you are running from God, please stop wasting not just your time, but also God's time. God will wait for you-wait you out, and there is a process that you must go through as well. My life's journey continued uninterrupted by dreams and visions, but I was also the person to whom many people turned to for advice. Many of my friends and peers would frequently come to me with unanswered questions, problems, and so much more. I suddenly became the go-to person.

Okay, let's see who caught that; yes, I was able to influence other people's children; and yes, spirits do transfer and manifest. Daily, parents cover and pray for your children! I spent my early teenage years in nightclubs and had access to places that were solely for adults. I could dress up, style my hair, and apply makeup to appear older and pass for an adult. Unlike now, they did not require proof of age; simply appearing to be of age was enough to gain access.

"Train up a child in the way he should walk, and when he is old, he will not depart from it," says Proverbs 22:6 King James Version (KJV).

Yes, even after everything my praying and anointed mother had taught and instilled in me, I still had a mind of my own. You must understand that "the greater the call, the earlier the devil begins his fight against you" and it all starts with the mind. Yes, it is about the mind. When Satan sees something great in you, he begins attacking your thoughts right away. As a child, he makes every effort to shut you down. So, keep a watchful eye on your children and the attacks on them. You must be aware of the devil's tools. We are not immune to attacks, and neither are your children. "Lord, cover the minds of all children, protect them from all evil". A daily prayer for and over your children is essential, as is a prayer against and from every hurt, harm, and danger.

Parents, you cannot change or even attempt to change a behavior unless you genuinely understand the source or root of the behavior. You should know your child better than anyone else, and when something changes, it should get and retain your undivided attention.

Please do not wait until things get out of control or something traumatic occurs. These are times when we all must watch and pray.

I had been introduced to the nightclub life, and I enjoyed hanging out in them. The devil obviously was working on me in such a way that I would tell my mother that I had an away game, which meant that I would have to leave the city and that I would be arriving home late, which was often the truth; but I started using it even when the games or track meets were local. Satan and his imps can obtain and gain legal scriptural ground to rob, kill, steal, and destroy through sin; so, the battle begins.

I started using this to stay out late at the club. I had a strategy, one that worked for a while before becoming an obsession. I wasn't doing anything wrong; I just wanted to dance and have fun. The devil was using a small thing to destroy everything God had planned and ordained for my life. I liked to dance and wondered if I would ever be able to do just that. I could dance the carpet off the floor, dance a hole in the floor; but this too was a trick of the devil. The devil will use anything that is not of God to his advantage.

So please, allow me to be perfectly clear in my saying that "The decisions we make are vital and can be life changing or deadly".

I became a prisoner of this thing. I started lying to my mother about having games or track meets when, in reality, I was packing that clean uniform in my gym bag with my clubbing clothes. Remember that Satan is the "Father of lies," and I was lying to my mother. I would even leave home dressed for a sporting event, but I had designated areas where I could change and transition into the dance queen. I was preoccupied with going to a nightclub. Let me tell you that some of the things I saw and witnessed during my visits to the club were things that even some adults should not have seen, yet I saw them as a teenager! Let me pause here and ask you a question. What is your relationship with God like? My prayer is that you have an intimate relationship with God. Second, how is your relationship with your child, up close and personal, is my prayer. So that we are clear and open in such a way that they can come and share and discuss everything, anything.

I may have had the looks of a young woman, but I had the mind of a child. I saw and witnessed people die in and outside of clubs, one that I knew I shouldn't be in but was always there. The person who was killed was someone who always kept me safe, he would make sure, that I did not consume alcohol, use drugs, or be harassed by any of the big boys, often known as "Pimps," on the streets.

I witnessed him being stabbed to death right in front of my eyes. It slowed my clubbing to a crawl, especially at that club; (not knowing that everything would be necessary in my spiritual growth and that it all was predestined by God!). That incident was an awakening to the truth that I should have never been there. God will take care of you, cover you, when you cannot or know how to. *"Romans 8:28 Says and we know that all things work together for good to them that love God, to them who are the called according to His purpose".*

I couldn't bear passing by the building because it hurt so much. I'd break down and cry myself to sleep. That night, I followed my routine: changed my clothes before going home and even remembering to clean my face but, the next morning my mother asked me questions, she had never asked me before. Due to lack of transportation or because one of my brothers needed to use the car for work, my mother was unable to constantly attend or be present at my games.

That morning, she knew something wasn't right with me. My mother knew because she had a strong-covenant relationship with the Lord, she had the gift of discernment and a mother's intuition. She said, "I had the look of death in my eyes." I never told her the truth about what happened that night, about what I saw and witnessed.

After my friend was laid to rest, I became the victim of rape not once, but twice within a year, something he had always shielded me from. I knew my violators and knew that if my friend was alive, not only would there be trouble for them both, but I might lose one or more of my brothers because we were a close net family and five of the eight were male. I was also terrified that it would destroy my mother. People are subjected to horrible acts such as sexual abuse through no fault of their own, but God's Grace and Mercy are sufficient!

I do not want to get ahead of myself in mentioning my non-profit organization, but this will serve as the moment that I shall enlighten you on being a survivor of rape. Allow me first to say that each individual victim of sexual assault has their own personal and private experience, I felt worthless, powerless, and out of control; I was afraid, embarrassed, ashamed and had times of emotional numbness. I felt so dirty, like there was something wrong with me. I wondered if people would be able to tell that I had been raped.

What would people think and say? To be honest, I've discovered that a person's remark can be just as painful as the original abuse, if not more so. I was mostly in denial and guilty-self-blame. I felt like I did something to make it happen, but the question for me was not where my friend was, but where God was. Why didn't God intervene?

There are some things in life that you just must let go of and move on, but this was not one of them, and the anger began to build. Sexual abuse is frequently used by the devil to transfer spirits: spirits of perversion, lust, promiscuity, sexual coldness, suicidal thoughts, and much more.

In most cases, you would never guess who has been abused. Sexual abuse is a very difficult subject to address, more so than most others. It evokes a terrible feeling of shame in both the speaker and the listener. I'm finding now that if I ask directly, some past victims are willing to admit it without shame or fear of being shunned or rejected. Most abused persons build walls around and inside their hearts that keep them from being happy; this is due to the fear of further hurt. I felt a range of emotions, but mostly I wanted to know why and why God would allow this to happen.

I considered suicide, but all I could think of was the anguish and pain it would cause my mother and, yes, my father. Okay, I wasn't only my mother's baby; I was also my father's girl and baby. My father left our home before I was a teenager, but I always made time and found a way to see him! I loved my daddy! Whatever he had, I was going to get some of it, whether it was food, money, and especially his time.

What kept me from taking my life was the thought of not wanting to leave a legacy for my mother and father that I had killed myself. Despite my pain, I decided to link myself to the reality of what it would be like for them, and I found the strength and fire to fight for my life, as well as theirs. My parents would have died of the shock, their baby girl!

Suicide is a "spirit," one of many spiritual beings of death and violence that plague humans all over the world. I struggled with suicidal thoughts. There were moments when taking my own life seemed like a good way out. "I can always take my life and escape the pain," I told myself, but it was a spiritual, emotional, and mental attack; the result of "Unprocessed Pain"! I couldn't get my head around the trauma I'd gone through. This was a spiritual attack, which is not uncommon. I was fleeing from the Lord and fighting the devil. If you are battling suicidal thoughts, I want to remind you that not all your thoughts are your own!

There is no single cause for suicide. Suicide most often happens when stressors and health issues converge to create an experience of hopelessness and despair. Depression is the most common condition associated with suicide, and it is often undiagnosed or untreated. Conditions like depression, anxiety, and substance problems, especially when un-addressed, increase the risk for suicide.

Struggling to cope with certain difficulties in your life can lead to suicidal thoughts. These difficulties may include mental health issues, bullying or discrimination, including racism, various types of abuse, such as domestic, sexual, physical, and spiritual abuse, bereavement, losing a loved one to suicide, the end of a relationship, long-term physical pain, or illness, adjusting to a major change, such as retirement or redundancy, money issues.

If you are contemplating suicide, I want you to know that your life is valuable. You are cherished! In the same way that I've had a breakthrough in my battle against suicidal spirits, I want you to know that you can, too!

There is still hope for you today because the truth is that God is with us in this trial! He will not abandon you or leave you. If the devil tempted Jesus to commit suicide, there is no shame in your temptation! You are not the object of your temptation. You are exactly who God says you are!

My heart goes out to anyone who has been personally affected by suicide or who has had a loved one or friend struggle with suicidal thoughts. My prayer is that the Holy Spirit will rest on you, your loved one, or a friend, and that peace will fill your hearts. Finally, please get some assistance; please!!! Healing, restoration, and deliverance are your portion.

Let me continue my story, I knew that if I told anyone, then someone was possibly going to die, and it could be one of my brothers. All I could see was at least three of them jumping into a car and leaving together all against the will of my mother. Then, later there being a knock at the door; and that knock would be that of the police in search of my brothers. So, I never told anyone, I realized that I was not only being watched for safety reasons, but also for other reasons unknown to me.

Recovering from sexual assault takes time, and the healing process can be painful; but you can regain your sense of control, rebuild yourself-worth, and learn to heal.

One in five women in the U.S. are raped or sexually assaulted at some point in their lives, often by someone they know and trust.

The impact of sexual violence goes far beyond any physical injuries; the trauma of being raped or sexually assaulted can be shattering, leaving you feeling scared, ashamed, and alone or plagued by nightmares, flashbacks, and other unpleasant memories. The world doesn't feel like a safe place anymore; you no longer trust others or even yourself. You may question your judgment, self-worth, and even your sanity. You may blame yourself for what happened or believe that you're dirty or damaged goods. Relationships feel dangerous, intimacy impossible and on top of that, like many rape survivors, you may struggle with PTSD, anxiety, and depression.

If you are a survivor of rape or sexual abuse, please report the violation and reach out to someone you trust for support. It is common to think that if you don't talk about your rape, it didn't really happen. But you cannot heal when you are avoiding the truth; hiding only adds to feelings of shame. As scary as it is to open up, it will set you free.

However, it is important to be selective about who you tell, especially at first. Your best bet is someone who will be supportive, empathetic, and calm. If you do not have someone you trust, talk to a therapist, or call a rape crisis hotline.

CHAPTER 2

"THE CHARGE" FIGHTING FROM A "SECRET PLACE"

I spent a lot of time at home in a secret place trying to figure out how could not only I, but God allow what happened to me happen. I even spent time trying to come up with a way possibly to get done what my brothers would have done by myself. I had my own agenda. I went through a great deal of emotions. I even stayed closer to home for a while and when I did go out, I was armed with a large switch blade. I also hung out with people that I felt had my back, being that of a Haitian Girl named Mariette and a Cuban Girl named Mariana; and yes, we all carried large switch blades and straight razors.

My days were half days during my Junior and Senior years of high school, and I was enrolled in the "Work Program," where I worked for limited hours during the school week. Every summer, I would work on the summer work programs. I had a dream and a plan to be "Happy, Healthy, and Wealthy" one day. I vowed that I would never be "poor" again.

I worked in the records department at the local city hall and at the local police department, answering and dispatching non-emergency calls. I went on to finish high school, start working, and enroll in college to pursue a career. I became involved with an older gentleman, and after some time, I found myself married to him and bearing his children. The relationship began improperly because I was looking for a Savior who I already had but failed to recognize and reach out to for the help I needed. *Proverbs 18: NKJV says, "He who finds a wife finds a good thing and obtains favor from the LORD"*. This was truly not the case. I did not know God's plan for me regarding marriage.

"Unhealed hurts and unresolved issues" troubled me. My marriage was a violent one; yes, we fought physically, with me frequently reaching for weapons. My husband was a cheater; he had the phone numbers of several women in his wallet, all frequently calling my house. His partner in crime let the cat out of the bag mistakenly after I had given birth to our first child; I was standing beside the door when I overheard them talking about going to meet some women. The partner in crime had assumed I was still in the hospital, healing from childbirth.

My marriage was over at that point. I needed peace and forgiveness for my troubled marriage, and restoration was desperately needed at this point.

Let me make you smile. My neighbor told me that she and her nephew would go to the store for snacks before coming home because they knew there would be some kind of action, a show, that weekend. They called it "Movie Night" at the time. Don't get me wrong: I continued to pray and attend church with my babies, but not with my family. Yes, my husband did not accompany us to church.

The marriage experienced major turbulence, which resulted in my exit and the dissolution of the marriage. But the most upsetting thing was being told by my soon-to-be ex-husband that despite all the hell I had been through in the marriage, one of my family members, a brother, had told him not to let me take his house. Once again, a dagger was thrust straight through my heart. It took me back to the time when I was raped and beaten repeatedly. The pain was excruciating, and it was applied by blood. I had to revert to that secret place and hide. A storm was brewing over my life; hurt, shame, rejection, and deception came from all directions.

The family bond had been completely severed, at this point.

I was so filled with rage and bitterness that I wanted nothing to do with him. Life seemed unfair and unjust; the pain caused by a family member was too much for me to bear. I tried everything I could think of, but nothing seemed to help; the pain only got worse. The only place I could find peace was in a secret place, isolation, or seclusion, but I continued my path of enjoying life as I felt I was.

How many of you reading this, are aware that I was not having an enjoyable time as I presented outwardly? It was "Pain misunderstood", the anger, resentment, the strife; I even felt rejection; and what I did not know was "It was all working for my good". I simply began dating King Pin men who showered me with money and gifts and began doing things that brought in fast money, which could have caused me to lose my freedom for a long period of time, if not the rest of my life. Even after I heard God's voice and was given specific instructions on what I needed to do, I went through and completed the "Fire Academy" and graduated.

Yes, I had my eyes set on money careers, and they all appeared to be risky. I knew I wanted more, and I was willing to go to any length to have a better life than what I had. There was greater and I wanted it. I dreamt and thought of wealth that could give me the security I needed in myself and in life. I wanted to be 'Happy, healthy and wealthy!'

Listen, I understood Angels were assigned and dispatched to cover me daily. *John 14:14 KJV If ye ask any thing in my name, I will do it.* I prayed to the Lord to cover and protect me from all hurt, harm, and danger. This became a daily prayer request for me. "Whoever has my commands and obeys them, he is the one who loves me. He who loves me will be loved by my Father, and I too will love him and show Myself to him."

In the midst of all that I had gone through and experienced, God knew my heart. The Bible agrees that God knows your heart. *God said to Samuel that He sees not as man sees, "Man looks on the outward appearance, but the Lord looks on the heart" (1 Samuel 16:7).* The Lord will also give you the desires of your heart: *Delight yourself in the LORD and he will give you the desires of your heart Psalm 37:4).*

He will make your righteousness shine like the dawn, the justice of your cause like the noonday sun. Be still before the LORD and wait patiently for him; do not fret when men succeed in their ways, when they carry out their wicked schemes.

There are some key words in that scripture; "Wait" was one

of them for me. I didn't know the word completely, and I didn't want to wait. I was young, and no, I was not reading the Bible as much as I should have been. I went to church because I knew it was the right thing to do and because I was raised in the church. My relationship with God had deteriorated. I was at war within myself and with the devil, who wanted to kill me because he had figured out my destiny, and God had a protective hedge around me because of his predetermined destiny for my life. I had a date with "Destiny," but I was enduring "Spiritual Warfare. I was in a war between my creator, my flesh, and the devil.

"Memoirs of a Rising Trafficking Queen Pin"

As I stated I started dating drug kingpins and soon found myself making runs-trafficking low-small quantities of drugs that grew into large quantities. The runs and the weight got bigger and bigger, while the money got bigger and better. This became my new "Hustle" and source of in-come. I'd go so far as to call myself a "Queen Pin" and no one knew. Yes, I was the most important female player in my ring-organization. The "Runners-Light Weights" were being busted in alarming numbers, and it was "uncommon" for women to be traffickers at the time. It was fairly common among young African American men. I could identify a "Runner " and a "King Pin" when I met or saw one.

It began as a trial run but grew to be much larger than I had anticipated. It went from someone else telling me what and when to move to me saying yes but handling the details myself. The less anyone knew about the game, the better, and the risk was lower. I never moved or rolled anything the same way twice. I followed my first mind, as they used to say back then. I never told the left hand what the right hand was up to.

I took control of what I was doing and moving. My words were always, "I Got This," and I always delivered. I quickly learned the game and found ways to change some things that I thought were a red flag. I found myself planning alternate routes and doing other things. I never drank coffee, but I did buy freshly ground coffee, black pepper, and Vaseline; and plenty of it. On rare occasions, I even used "cow manure" as a tool. I did everything I could to "cover-protect" myself, including keeping my mouth shut and not telling anyone.

The boss went from questioning me to not questioning me. I had no idea I was making big things happen in a big way. My job was to get from point "A" to point "B" with ease with no problems and I made that happen every time. I used everything to my advantage because I was a very attractive young woman with the whole package. I could rock any pair of jeans, no matter the brand, and I adored fitted overalls. I made a point of looking and smelling nice depending on the occasion. I'd sold my soul to the devil, and I was all in to win it. So, if you're sinning and having fun with it, you have sold your soul to the devil-satan.

I always had large sums of money, and I had two luxurious automobiles with nice rims. Some people always thought they were a man's automobiles, but they soon realized that this was not the case. I had and loved Gucci bags, watches, and belts that I was either given or bought for myself. I loved the thought of being able to go into a store and purchase what I wanted. But I continued to hear God's voice and feel the tug. But how do you let go of a life like this, especially when you had not had it like this before?

The money was quick and good, but the voice, which occasionally became audible, was extremely loud. But the devil is aware of your preferences and desires; as put by the King James Version, "For the love of money is the root of all evil: which while some coveted after, they erred from the faith, and pierced themselves through with many sorrows." I didn't love money, but I thought I could compensate for what I lacked as a child by providing a better life for my children.

My daughter competed in numerous beauty pageants, winning, and bringing home six feet trophies and checks. I wanted more, and my funds were being used to pay for the dresses and other items required for her to enter and compete. The quick money paid the bills, and yes, I did pay my tithes at church and believed what the Bible said about tithing. Tithing has numerous benefits: the reaping and sowing law.

"We Are Blessed When We Give Tithes and Offerings", is what my mother taught me. "Bring ye all the tithes into the storehouse, that there may be meat in mine house, and prove me now here with ... if I will not open you the windows of heaven, and pour you out a blessing, that there shall not be room enough to receive it" (Malachi 3:10).

Followers of the Lord's words are encouraged to give the Lord a tithe of their fruits, wealth, or bounty. Tithing is regarded as an expression of gratitude to the Lord in both the Old and New Testaments. This is what my mother taught me as a child, and she gave me money to practice it.

I went to a night club with a good friend named "Tee" one

night. Yes, a nightclub. I carried on with the night scene, but on a different level. The clothes, jewelry, and money changed, but I was always with Tee, my close friend. We'd ride out and get the Big Ballers' attention. We never had to spend any money in Miami because the Ballers always took care of the tabs. We were always ladies, divas. Please allow me to define the term "Diva".

"A self-important person who is temperamental and difficult to please," defines a Diva. One who is a glamorous fashion diva, particularly a popular female (typically used of a woman). When you "look good, you feel good," I'd often heard, so, I had always wanted to look and feel good. Perhaps in my next book, I'll dive deeper into some of the things we could force a man to do while slow dancing on the dance floor. But on this night, I was approached by a strange man I didn't know, who whispered something in my ear, and his words were both shocking and frightening the kind of fear that could paralyze a person; the kind of fear that was now causing a problem in my life.

My girlfriend asked if I knew him, and I told her that I didn't, but that he was just trying to hit on me, implying that he had an interest in me. I walked away from her to speak with him but stayed within her line of sight. No, she had no idea what I was doing. I often called her "green", meaning "clueless". Yes, we were close, but some things are never revealed, especially when committing a crime. Loose lips sink ships, which means you've just told on yourself to the law. I was afraid that if I told her, she'd slip and tell someone, which would be my downfall.

What this man said to me was the single most important thing that influenced my decision to stop trafficking. This man made me an offer that I could never have imagined, but it was an offer that I refused. Who was he? And how did he find out what he thought he knew? What mattered most to me though was that he knew! As he left, I told my girl, "Let's go, I am hungry, some people you just don't deal with. I only want to be happy, healthy, and wealthy."

I fought various thoughts in my head and refused to consider walking away. Thoughts of going to jail or dying crossed my mind, but I quickly dismissed them! I had made a name for myself as someone who could get the job done. "A Mover and Shaker" was how I described myself. Nothing was moved until I was comfortable with my timing and the "color" codes. But let me tell you that he was only the messenger for someone bigger than himself. Yes, that's right; only a messenger for someone "bigger". He not only came with a message, but he also came with what he said was a gift of appreciation for my good work, which was placed in my hand when he took my hand upon his approach.

Everyone talks about money, because they lack it; some want to make more, while others are simply obsessed with it. It has always been this way, but making money appears to be the main goal on everyone's 'to do' list these days. Money is merely a means to an end. We require it for many things to live and survive. But we must never forget that there is so much more to life. "Make that money, but don't let it make you," I often heard in my world. "Do not get caught Up"!

Before destruction, there is a warning. I was presented with an offer that I should not have been able to refuse, but there are some things you just don't touch; fear of both the known and the unknown drove me. I could be "set for life," or this could be a "set up," but I didn't want any part of it, it was too good to be true for me, and the risk was even greater; I couldn't comprehend what had been offered to me. All I could hear was "No" and "Run!" Listen, the choices we make in life are significant. The choices you make will eventually lead you somewhere. Some roads are "Dead Ends," others are a waste of time, and still others can lead to regret, sorrow, and even death.

As previously stated, we need money, some are for things we've never had, while others are for necessities; whatever your goal, whether you like it or not, money is a big part of your life. We should strive for a better today for ourselves and our families if we remember that we are here to make each minute count and money is not everything. I'm so glad I got delivered!!!

"My Awakening to Truth"

I didn't understand what I now understand because I didn't have anyone to help me understand what I was hearing, seeing, and experiencing; thus, I continued my path of running away from what I was hearing. Please allow me to pause for a moment to remind you that even while I was running, God always confirmed his word by sending that same woman, JoAnne Marshall Brunson, who would always remind me of who I was and that I had been chosen by God.

Please understand that every time I saw this woman approaching, I would jump into the backseats of cars, hide behind cars, buildings, and people in short, I would do anything to keep myself out of her sight, yet she reminded me whenever she saw me; I'm sure you get the idea. But, believe me, I thought I'd gotten away, but there was another, yes, another. I was completing the "Emergency Medical Technical Course" (EMT) when another was sent out to reel me in. She came when I was alone and in the secret place, even when you can't see or feel God, He is walking along side you or carrying you.

Even after trying to run from the Lord, I found myself reconnecting with someone who was also connected to and had an intimate relationship with God; her name was Bettie Green, and she took me to church with her. Every now and then, she would pay a visit to an older saint who had preached the Gospel for many years and had reached out to the people through the power of God. I was brought before this woman, whose name was Mother Corine Manuel, and this woman of God began to minister to me about some of the things I had experienced and gone through. She also began to speak into my life about what God was going to do in my life, and to confirm what Joanne had previously spoken about.

She told me that the Lord had called me and chosen me before I was born. She began to pray for and over me, and as she did so, she placed her hands on my head, and I felt something I had never felt before. I fell to the ground, and it was an experience I will never forget. She touched me three times, and the anointing of GOD slayed me. Yes, I fell, and the rest is truly unexplainable! No, I was not pushed, this feeling was real, and something was happening to me; I saw things flash before my eyes.

The Anointing is the supernatural power used for supernatural assignments; it is a heavenly electric power. Men and women will see and recognize the power of God's anointing on you if you are connected to that power. The anointing is the liquid power that comes with the Holy Spirit's manifestation.

The anointing prepares God's people to receive the endowment of "Power from on high" promised in an earlier 1831 revelation. At the present time, any holder of the Melchizedek priesthood may anoint the head of an individual by the laying on of hands. Jesus was smeared with the anointing specifically the person, presence, and power of the Holy Spirit. Isaiah 10:27 describes the anointing as the burden-removing, yoke destroying power of God. The anointing is what delivers God's people and sets the captives free.

After God released me from lying face down, I ran back to

the car I had been driven in and asked the driver to take me home. I was called back into the house and much of the same continued and I was told thatI had a kingdom calling upon my life. I had no idea what that meant, but I knew it was serious because this woman was serious, and so was the power she wielded. That night, the Holy Spirit came upon me and gave me the gift of speaking in tongues.

I was taken home to have another all-night encounter with the Lord in the secret place; this time lying face down or flat on my back looking up but unable to move, just wailing and travailing in the Spirit with this new gift of tongues, I needed to know what had clearly just occurred. Speaking in tongues, also known as "Glossolalia," is the practice of people uttering words or speech-like sounds, which are often thought by believers to be languages unknown to the speaker.

God does more than save us from sin and death when we profess faith in Jesus Christ. He saves us for dynamic service within His ministry arm—the global church, the Body of Christ, His Kingdom. The Holy Spirit dispenses spiritual gifts, at the direction of the Father to empower every believer so that we can effectively contribute to the growth and vitality of the Body of Christ-His Kingdom (1 Corinthians 12:4-11). One of the most controversial Holy Spirit gifts since Pentecost has been "Speaking in Tongues."

What are these tongues exactly? As with most Biblical topics, the first mention should guide our interpretation of the topic as it appears elsewhere in the Bible. The Early Church began to speak in tongues after the Holy Spirit descended at Pentecost (Acts 2:4). These tongues were actual spoken languages bestowed by the Holy Spirit, allowing the Gospel to transcend language and cultural barriers (Acts 2:5-12).

There is only one Truth. God is light and in Him, there is no darkness, deception or lies. When the truth has been opened to them, you can now say that truth has been revealed, now comes the change! Listen, the spiritual realm exists; it is a real, unseen existence that is alive and active; satan and his evil and demonic imps (spirits) are at war with God and His angels; the war is about the "possession of your soul, mind, will and emotions. Satan wishes to dominate a person's unredeemed spirit; that of you and me.

The Bible tells the story of the world's creation, humanity's fall, and God's plan to reconcile the world to Himself through the death and resurrection of Jesus. It goes on to explain the church's responsibility to go into the whole world and make disciples (Matthew 28:19–20).

The story of humanity's fall introduces us to the devil, also known as satan, and the forces he has unleashed on the world. These forces were in charge of tempting humankind to deviate from God's will (Genesis 3) and have worked to undermine God's every plan.

The Bible repeatedly portrays the world as a war zone, with humans caught in the crossfire between God and His enemy, Satan, keep this in mind.

There was a time when I was divorced from my husband. I was in school, living in a townhouse with no lights and eating from a Styrofoam cooler, and satan was battling me from every angle and end. I had found out a few weeks before that I was expecting another child. I'm not lying when I say I did not sleep all night. I walked to class the next day because my car was broken down and being repaired and I lived about a half mile from the college. As I had an evening class, I would always arrive early enough to get something hot to eat from the cafeteria's grill before it closed for the evening. But how could it be that I was who these people say I am while going through pure hell?

Let me share with you an experience I had; one night on my way home from class, in the dark, with some light, because there was distance between the streetlights. A car pulled up and I was armed with a knife and at the time, a gun. The voice I recognized was that of my professor, and he inquired as to where I was going and why was walking. I told him I was a few feet from home and that my car was being repaired. But he noticed the remains of my food and asked if there was anything else I needed to tell him. I told him no and his response was "are you sure". I told him I was pregnant, and he asked why I had not told him. My response was that I was afraid of being kicked out of the program because it was an Emergency Medical Technicians course that required practical or hands-on training.

This man read me the riot act about not telling him I was pregnant, walking alone at night, my living situation, and so on. This man made sure to ask if I had eaten each night before class, and some nights we had food, he assisted in getting my power restored, and he made sure to in-form the class about my pregnancy.

"But God shall supply", everyone has value and worth in God's Eyes; when I couldn't see a way, God made one. I was called and chosen, but before I could come forth, I had to endure and come through the process first.

"The CHARGE"

I had several more encounters with Mother Manuel, who has since gone to be with the Lord (Rest in Peace General), and one of her closest friends, Mother Apostle Betty White, both of whom were pivotal in exposing God's will for my life. My life was never the same after meeting these two powerful women of God, true mothers in Zion; they were the type to tell you to yield, to come out of sin and live a holy life. *I beseech you therefore, brethren, by the mercies of God, that ye present your bodies a living sacrifice, holy, acceptable unto God, which is your reasonable service (Romans 12:1.)* They clearly told you what the Lord said. To be "broken," I had to be "broken". Some people, places, and things had to go, things from the outside world. I was instructed to consecrate myself, sanctify myself, and set myself apart for God's service. They told me to yield and say yes to God.

They spoke with God's authority and had no problem

explaining why; and in the end, you had to seal every prophecy.

It appears to have triggered something extremely powerful within me; It gave me a drive I had never had before. It was like there was a fire burning deep within and it resulted in a significant change in my life my mind, soul, and body were all renewed. They both placed a "Charge" into and over my life that I received and accepted and sealed with the laying on of hands.

I couldn't get enough of trying to feel the Holy Spirit's presence. Hey, there's an old song that goes, "You can't hurry God, you just have to wait;" I wasn't trying to rush God, but rather to make Him wait, which obviously did not work. I was well on my way to becoming empowered. My problems remained in the midst of all his splendor and glory, and I saw no way out, but He did. I found myself making a vow to The Lord during one of my most intimate and personal encounters with Him. I vowed to go wherever He told me to go, to do whatever He told me to do, and to say whatever He told me to say, if He would just set me free and get me out of the mess, I was in.

That is exactly what the Lord did. The Lord first had to

deliver me from myself as I was and had been on a road of self-destruction. The Lord saved my life and rescued me. He delivered me from my flesh and satan. I got through it all by the Grace of God, not by my own goodness, but by and through the Grace of God.

God not only remembered me, but also reminded and showed me exactly where the money I had buried under the doghouse at my ex-husband house and some that I had hidden at my mother's house. I was learning and growing in "Grace". You will not grow if you stop learning. 2 Timothy 4:1-5 says, I charge you in the presence of God and of Christ Jesus, who is to judge the living and the dead, and by his appearing and his kingdom: preach the word; be ready in season and out of season; reprove, rebuke, and exhort, with complete patience and teaching. For the time is coming when people will not endure sound teaching but having itching ears they will accumulate for themselves teachers to suit their own passions, and will turn away from listening to the truth and wander off into myths. As for you, always be sober-minded, endure suffering, do the work of an evangelist, fulfill your ministry.

In ministry, you will be judged more strictly, both by the Lord and by the congregation. People will look to you as a role model for the church and the world. People will look to you for guidance; they will look to you for solace, advice, and correction. My charge to you is the same as Paul's charge to Timothy: First and foremost, we are charged before God to preach the Word. People want your experience-testimony as well as your wisdom; the people want your charm. But, above all, they require God's sufficient Word so; never, ever refuse to give it to them without making any compromise.

Paul's qualifier is also important: preach the word both in and out of season. The Word is very much in season right now, but that may not be the case in the future; y our leadership cannot be held responsible for this. In the outside world, and even in many churches, the word is out of season. You might find yourself in a church or community where the word is out of season one day. The charge to you is to cling to God's Word and the gospel of Jesus, which it proclaims to be "of First Importance."

Your "Charge" before God is to lead His people both firmly and patiently. Remember that you must be accountable and keep your mind focused on Christ's obedience so that you can take every thought captive. By God's grace, you must strive for sexual purity in your marriage and in your mind; you must prioritize God and your family. Be serious about soul winning and healing, about fellowship, visitation, and counseling. You must be sober minded about the fate of sinners.

Your preaching and ministry will only be as effective as your prayer life; always, always, always keep JESUS and His Life at the center of everything you preach, teach, and practice!!! What is the point if it isn't saturated with Jesus and focused on Jesus? Who would benefit from it? Pay attention to yourself, to your teaching and to your way of life. In ministry, self-awareness is your most powerful ally. I will shift right here, Paul says ENDURE, remember this!!!

CHAPTER 3

"THE MANDATE"

My release came with the birth of my last child and my relocation to Georgia, where the Lord began to truly manifest Himself in my life by allowing me to hear His voice more clearly. But satan, of course, fought back by putting all of the fleshly things I liked in easy reach. This was Atlanta, so I had to see the city and, of course, the night life. I found myself back in the clubs, some nights; I would find myself club-hopping between three different clubs in a single night. We always valet parked and sat in the VIP section of the clubs. We ate at some of Atlanta's best restaurants.

I was introduced to Atlanta Hawks and Falcons games, concerts, and activities, as well as all the high-end clothing and jewelry stores. I was having the time of my life. I got my own place and soon discovered that temptation was knocking at the door. I began to see satan, the devil, through a deceptive lens because he is the father of lies and a deceiver. He had come to set me up to bring me down, and he was using anyone and everything to do so.

The devil, also known as Satan, is a real spiritual

being with real power and a destructive agenda. He is God's enemy, and thus the enemy of all God's people. He is mentioned in seven different books of the Old Testament of the Bible. And he is mentioned by all nine New Testament writers. He is a real adversary that we must be aware of; as *1 Peter 5:8 states, "the devil roams around like a roaring lion, seeking whom he may devour."* Satan is far more powerful than we give him credit for. The Apostle Paul refers to him as the "prince of the power of the air" in Ephesians 2. He wields significant power and authority over our current world system, as well as significant influence over people all over the world. And everything he does, along with his demonic army of fallen angels, whom I refer to as "Imps," is to undermine God's good and perfect plan for humanity.

We need to be aware of the devil's influence and plans in this world; *Ephesians 6:11 KJV says, "Put on the whole armor of God, that ye may be able to stand against the wiles of the devil"*.

Satan knew I had one foot in the Kingdom and one foot out of it: the Body of Christ and hell, so he sent in what I called reinforcements. He sent in someone from my past, a king pen drug dealer from Florida who was now living in Atlanta. The Devil was preparing me to fail, but I passed the test. For a time, the king pen was my roommate, but I made it clear that the number one rule was that no drugs were to be brought into my home, and that if I ever suspected or discovered drugs in my home, he would have to find another place to live.

I thought I was doing well because, as he had previously stated in our discussions about the rules of my home, he would almost never be there as the resident. I only saw him three or four times a month. He would only come in on weekends to sleep, shower, and change clothes. Please don't let me forget to eat, which he is capable of doing. I had no objections to this because he paid half of all bills, and it went to his paying for everything.

He would call ahead of time to see what was for Sunday dinner, and if it wasn't what he wanted, he'd ask if I'd go to the market and get whatever he wanted, and he'd refund me the cost.

I found myself becoming a chef in my own home, which I didn't mind because I was getting paid to do it and I was eating well; really well. He would order oxtails, short ribs, steaks, shrimp, and lobster. I made a lot of collard greens, seven cheese macaroni and cheese, potato salad, and yes, my banana pudding and peach cobbler because he liked soul food; my mother again taught and trained me in the kitchen. He only brought a female friend or companion over for dinner a few times, with advance notice and approval; something that had to be discussed and within the rules of my home.

But let me tell you that the woman ate more than he did; I know the food was good because she asked for more than just seconds; she asked for takeout. For weeks, I teased him, and we laughed about it, but he never brought her back. Things began to deteriorate when he began arriving home drunk and throwing up on the bathroom floor.

I'd clean everything up and get him into bed, with him sleeping all day and having no idea how he got home. When I went out to his car, the door was open; there were bottles of Dom Perignon all over the seats, and large sums of money on the floor.

I told him that he was living dangerously and that this was a sign that he was slipping. When you're in the "Game" as a King Pin", you can't slip. You adhere to the basic rules to the letter. This means no drugs in your personal vehicles or on you, no speeding, no driving while intoxicated, and no drama with anyone that will draw attention to yourself. Remember that the time I spent in the game taught me a lot of things, including the importance of always having a strategy or plan in place and never being predictable. Despite this, I continued to pray and hear the Lord's voice.

I remember calling him one weekend to see if he was coming home for dinner because he hadn't been there in a long time. He asked if he needed to, and I said yes, but I had a word of caution for him from the Lord. He arrived, but he was not alone; he was accompanied by a young woman and a child, whom he asked to stay with me until he could find a place for them.

I made them feel welcome and invited him into my room for a private conversation. We were clear on the woman and child because it was his child, but I needed to tell him what the Lord had shown me. I told him that warning comes before destruction, and this was his warning that someone was following him and had snitched on his operation. I told him everything about the vision and the Lord's words, and he was completely taken a back. He understood I was unaware of his operation, his associations with specific people, and their descriptions; all he could say to me is "How do you know this", my response was "It's The Word of The Lord, I don't know anything other than what the Lord has given me to tell you," I told him.

I don't want to dwell on it too long, but it all ended with him disappearing and not returning my calls. Later, I discovered that the Lord's word had come true, and he was being held in jail on drug charges and conspiracy. A relative came to pick up the child, the mother and his remaining belongings. Yes, the Lord revealed to me that I had been watched and followed at times, and that the Feds and the local agency were aware that I had been clear and clean with only trips to church, the market, and job interviews.

I'd like to take a moment to thank someone who welcomed me and the new life that God had predestined for me in Atlanta. He was the vessel God had chosen to assist me in transitioning from Florida and settling in; Kenneth "Teddy Bear" Holmes is no longer among us on this earth, I remember the good times we had, the people, places, and new things you introduced me to, and most of all your laughter and love for God's people. I did not know that the day you called me over to see you off on a road trip home to Florida was your way of saying goodbye.

I could not stay in the community or county because I would have to pass your house, and the pain was too much for me. I relocated to Atlanta's Southside with a gaping hole in my heart and again asked God why; why had he taken you away from me. The fruit of the Spirit, according to the Bible, is "love, joy, peace, patience, kindness, generosity, faithful- ness, gentleness, and self-control." Those who are in Christ are distinguished from unbelievers in that they have been endowed with the Holy Spirit, enabling them to bear fruit. *1 Corinthians 13:13 NASB says, "But now faith, hope, and love remain, these three; but the greatest of these is love".*

This man loved and showed love to everyone that he met. He never met a stranger, no matter the race or nationality. You met him today; he was your friend tomorrow. He genuinely loved God's people. I Miss You So Much, Rest Well Sir.

God's presence was palpable in my new home and prayer rooms. I was so hungry and thirsty for God. Being in the presence of The Lord took on a greater significance. I had my sins washed by the Blood of Jesus and I wanted to have a new encounter with God. *"Blessed are those who hunger and thirst for righteousness, for they will be satisfied," says Matthew 5:6.* I'd walk around my house worshiping and praising God, there was a particular spot directly in front of the bathroom mirror where I felt the presence of God and I could not move. Any saved and unsaved person who would come to my house would say, "I felt something in your bathroom", with my reply being "That is the Presence of God".

Throughout that period of my life, I continued to pray to God and ask if I was who everyone said I was, why would He allow me to go through what I had gone through? How and why did He permit all of this to occur? I needed clarity and comprehension; I was always wondering why. God began to respond during my constant questioning.

For a very long time I would ask "Why me?" and never heard a thing, but one day He replied with "Why Not You"? If you are experiencing or facing a situation and are seeking an answer from God, let me tell you, I had not only to wait on God, I had to wait in God! Despite my circumstances, the Lord found me in a place of humility, praising and honoring Him.

I kept asking because I did not understand His response. "Why not you?" and "What about My Son?" were the only responses I received. I began to think and ponder about Christ's life to the point of asking God, "What does His life have to do with my being raped?" I begged the Lord to help me. When I say I was humbled, I mean it. God had my full attention. But what did He mean when He said, "Why Not Me"? Warfare!

Spiritual warfare is a battle against satan that occurs in an unseen, spiritual dimension and is fought with weapons that have divine power to destroy strongholds. This is all while resisting satan, remaining firm in your faith, and pursuing the ultimate victory of demolishing arguments against God's knowledge and taking captive every thought to make it obedient to Christ. From a Christian perspective, spiritual warfare exists within every child of God, between the Holy Spirit and the lusts of the carnal flesh.

It was 3:23 AM in the morning when God decided to get me up and out of bed and on my face to say, "That everything that you have gone through and will go through will not be for and about you; it will be for someone else". God's purpose and plan for my life became crystal clear to me at that point. When the people of God said that God would use me for His glory, I knew exactly what they meant. Yes, God had a plan for me even after all the hurt, pain, disappointment, and shame. God was and continues to be my saving grace.

I must pause to emphasize that being chosen by God has a cost, carrying a mantle for Christ is not an easy task. The anointing comes at a high cost, the anointing gives you power, but it comes at a price that most people are unwilling to pay!

Some even falsely walk under the anointing by accepting the call but failing to walk and live by a holy standard.

"Be Holy, for I Am Holy," says Leviticus 19:20, this passage documents the Lord's emphasis on holiness. In Hebrew, the word for Holy is "Qadash," which means to be sanctified, consecrated, and dedicated. *1 Peter 1:16; for it is written, "Be holy, because I am holy for, I am the LORD your God; consecrate yourselves, therefore, and be holy, because I am holy, you must not defile yourself with any crawling creature.*

We all have a past but when we come to Christ, He forgives our sins and makes us holy and blameless before God. The one thing we all have in common is our past; before we came to Christ, we were all rebellious, hostile, and separated from God; our sins, attitudes, and actions kept us from knowing our loving Heavenly Father. So even if you had been a "good person" before coming to Christ, you still had attitudes and thoughts that kept you from God. God did not wait for us to clean up our act before He began His work of salvation; while you were still in rebellion and hostile towards Him, He began working in your life to draw you to Himself. The Holy Spirit began speaking to your heart and bringing you to faith in Christ Jesus. Holy and Blameless you are in Christ, Jesus did away with the sinful nature, the past and present sins, and the rebellion against God. He broke down the wall between you and God through His death on the cross, gave you a new nature and sent the Holy Spirit to dwell in you.

If you are willing to pay the price, you must be prepared to make great sacrifices and go through great trials; the greater your trials, the greater the anointing." Listen, I was always praying, and I was taught to fast, but it was my suffering that drove me to meditate and go into isolation or seclusion. I needed more, more guidance in cultivating everything God had placed within me. I had to learn that I did not suffer to "pay a price for the anointing." I suffered, and I continue to suffer, because I WAS ANOINTED. I was fleeing something I did not understand. I also had to understand that God will create an illusion for the enemy to reveal himself, and that enemy was "me" at the time. Yes, I was sometimes my own worst enemy. I had to get out of not only God's way, but also my own—the spirit of self and flesh. I had to learn that the ANOINTING COMES THROUGH WARFARE. It comes through pain, suffering, trials, and afflictions.

Romans 8:28 says, "And we know that all things work together for good to them that love God, to them who are the called according to his purpose". Everything in my life that has taken place has its purpose. I am a firm believer that nothing happens that God does not allow.

In *Job 1:6-10;*

Verse 6 says, "Now there was a day when the sons of God came to present themselves before the Lord, and Satan came also among them".Satan is accountable and must answer to God.

Verse 7, "And the Lord said unto Satan, Whence comest thou? Then Satan answered the Lord, and said, from going to and fro in the earth, and from walking up and down in it". This verse shows accountability to God.

Verse 8, "And the Lord said unto Satan, Hast thou considered myservant Job, that there is none like him in the earth, a perfect and an upright man, one that feareth God, and escheweth evil"? Can God bring you before satan? What would you do? How would you handle this? Would you pass the test? Would you curse God?

Verse 9, "Then Satan answered the Lord, and said, Doth Job fear God for nought"? Do You Fear God?

Verse 10, "Hast not thou made a hedge about him, and about his house, and about all that he hath on every side? Thou hast blessed thework of his hands, and his substance is increased in the land".

I have often taken Jobs name out and replaced it with my name. I had to become a "Jobett!" Listen, do not you let nothing get in the way of your victory. God had begun a great work in me, and I knew that He would complete it. *Philippians 1:6; says "Being confident of this very thing, that He which hath begun a good work in you will perform it until that day of Christ Jesus."* I had been anointed for this life.

The liquid power that comes with the manifestation of the Holy Spirit is known as the anointing. The anointing is God's presence and power. How can you tell if you are God's anointed? You must be approachable and trustworthy.

If God has anointed you to minister to His people, you must be a people person; you must be kind and friendly so that people are not intimidated by you. You must also make them feel at ease sharing their thoughts and secrets with you.

You have the power to do good and heal all who are oppressed by the devil if you have been anointed with the Spirit and power of God. We have the authority to set captives free and carry out the work of the ministry that we inherited from the Lord, and our inheritance is among the sanctified (set apart). *John 14:12 "Truly, truly, I tell you, whoever believe on Me will also do the works that I do; and greater works than these will he do, because I am going to the Father."*

The more anointing I carried, the more warfare I faced from the kingdom of darkness. You must understand that before God can entrust His power to your life, you must have overcome something major that will serve as a testament to your life.

That is why, the moment you say "Yes" to God, you will experience unexplainable warfare that will make you want to give up.

NEVER TAKE A TRUE AND ANOINTED WOMAN OR MAN OF GOD FOR GRANTED, BECAUSE THEIR ANOINTING DID NOT COME CHEAP. People want the anointing, but they do not want to pay the price, the cost is our perfect obedience to God's word.

God's anointing is priceless, and we should never take it for granted or treat it casually. *"But the anointing that you have received from Him abides in you, and you do not need anyone to teach you; but as the same anointing teaches you concerning all things, and is true, and is not a lie, and you will abide in Him,"* (NKJV) 1 John 2:27

We cannot continue to carry God's holy anointing if we continue to sin. Much of what is happening in our lives, that is, our flesh is the direct result of demonic activity. We belong to God, so we should obey Him and live holy as He does. I had to learn that His anointing is never about me, It is by God's grace. He knew what kind of sinful life I had led, how my running felt to me like I was denying him, and how it was entirely by God's grace that God chose to use me in such an incredible way.

Your calling will require significant sacrifices from you, as well as some critical decisions, and your obedience will be critical in completing your kingdom assignment. When I realized all these, I repented and grieved my sins. I became incredibly grateful for the cross, as well as the grace, mercy, and favor that only God could have bestowed upon my life. God had to truly save me, for truth be told I was truly lost and needed to be found; I needed to be saved from myself.

I spent countless hours, laying prostrate, crying out, praying, and speaking to the Lord from that point forward. Let me tell you, nothing beats an up close and personal relationship with God; I mean getting intimate; yes, intimately giving God your entire being. Genesis 24:48 "And I bowed and prostrated myself to Jehovah, and I blessed Jehovah.

God was transforming me from the inside out! He was cleansing and pruning me, preparing me for battle; I was attending a private boot camp. When I prayed, all I can say is something always happened! When I called his name, He always came to me.

"If you cast your cares on Me, then I shall move," God began to say to me. *Psalm 55:22 KJV Says, Cast thy burden upon the Lord, and he shall sustain thee: he shall never suffer the righteous to be moved.* My prayers would always be "God help me to know and understand You more, take away my worries, cares, hurts and pain". I knew that He could fix everything, whatever you give to God, He will give it back greater.

The enemy was persistent, however, because all hell broke loose in my life, and I could not get off the wall or out of the secret place! I had to stay on that wall! After years of wondering why me, I came to a point in my life where I finally accepted the answers that the Lord had given me. My relationship had progressed to the point where I was completely in tune with God.

I was on fire for the Lord. God's purpose and plan for my life had become crystal clear to me, I was preaching about God to everyone. At this point in my life, evangelism was very strong. I had discovered myself in God, and He and His kingdom were within me. I had a firm grasp on the power and authority that had been bestowed upon me, and I was prepared to reclaim everything that the devil had stolen from me by force.

This meant that war and the devil would never be allowed to take away my pride, joy, or self-esteem again. But first, I had to clear my mind and humble myself, I had to network with Kingdom minded people who inspired me to want and complete the change, and of course, I had to work.

I had reached a point where I needed to know why he had allowed me to go through what I had gone through. I kept asking, and it wasn't until a Friday night after I had gone to bed that the Lord woke me up by saying, that He could now answer me because I was now grown enough in the spirit realm to understand His answer. I had asked God "Why me?" and received different answers each time, first there was no answer, then there was "Why not you?" and then "Why My Son?"

I pondered and considered those words in such a way that I knew I would never have been able to bear the cross" in the same way that Christ did, given that it was all for and about my sins! I could not have paid such a high price! I began to consider what the price of Jesus was. According to the Gospel of Matthew 26:15 in the New Testament, Judas Iscariot betrayed Jesus for thirty pieces of silver.

What or who would be the reason for my being sent to the cross? I am only speaking honestly when I say, "I would not have been able to remain on that cross" at that time in my life.

Remember that at 3:23 a.m., I was awakened on my face, prostrate before the Lord. The Lord told me that everything I had been through or would go through was not for or about me, but for and about someone else. That immediately took me to my secret place. When the Lord speaks, you must be completely still with no distractions. You know, I think now is a good time for me to tell you about where all my fighting took place. To this day, I can say that I have only had three physical fights in my life, all of which were minor with the exception of one where I had a knife pulled on me, but they fled after nicking my hand with the knife and I told her that I was going to beat the brakes off of her, I was in the flesh; but I meant business. This is not how we fight.

"Watch and pray, that ye enter not into temptation," Jesus instructed His disciples (Matthew 26:41). We can overcome sinful temptations through prayer.

Ask God to help you avoid making poor decisions, this will give you the strength to do the right thing. *Hebrews 4:12 says "For the Word of God is living and powerful, and sharper than any two-*

edged sword." Prayer is a powerful weapon that has been given to us; we, as Kingdom believers, need to utilize this amazing weapon we have been given.

"And whatever you ask in prayer, you will receive if you have faith," says Matthew 21:22. Mark 9:29 "This kind cannot be driven out by anything but by prayer." Jesus told them. *Mark 11:24 "So, whatever you ask for in prayer, believe that you have received it, and it will be yours."* Your words must be faith filled, meaning you must believe what you are saying. Faith is a gift from God, but it must be applied in your life. Somethings will require more than just a feeling to get you through, I had to pray my way through a lot of situations back then and now. Prayer is essential in everything and is your first ministry.

Now comes the juice, so remember what I said about my runs? Well, I had to work to support myself and my children, so my next runs were for UPS, yes, the "United Parcel Service".

I worked as a seasonal driver for UPS, driving a P1600 UPS truck. Every morning, I rolled out with the big boys—the senior drivers; I packed in long overtime hours and the pay wasn't great. When it was all over, I rolled on over to the DOC-The Georgia Department of Corrections. OK, I hear you asking, "What?" yes, corrections officer".

Wait, it doesn't end there; while at the DOC, I had previously applied at one or more of the local Sheriff's departments that had a hiring freeze in place. So, I got a call saying that the freeze had been lifted and that they wanted to know if I was still interested. I was hired as a DO-Detention Officer for about 30 days (about 4 1/2 weeks) and then sent directly to the Public Safety Law Enforcement Academy, for Law Enforcement Certification. Well, not only did I graduate first in my class, but I was also president of my graduating class. From hood trafficking to hood protection, would you say?

Yes, everything about me was legal; there was no more fast money. I was working and paying for everything that I needed and wanted. For some things I became the layaway queen, no more paying cash for everything.

It was time to build some things. I had prayed and asked the Lord to do something in my life, and He did exactly what He said He would do. I had my sights set on a certain prestige automobile and every time I saw one, I would say, "There goes my car", the car was a Mercedes Benz. One day, I was sitting on my patio when the Lord spoke to me and said, "Get up", I obeyed and drove to the dealership, which was not far from my home, per His instructions; and then I got out of my car and walked around the parking lot.

I looked at several cars until He said, "Black on Black". He reminded me of a prophecy spoken over me by Mother Annette McGuire at an evening church service and confirmed by Prophet Brian Mosley at another service. He stated that my new car had been released because of my obedience and faithfulness; after perusing the lot, I spotted a black on black near the door and He said, "That's it, that is your car". I took a test drive in the car and was told that we couldn't do much because it was late and that they would work on it the next day. I was told that I did not have bad credit, but rather a low score that needed to be improved.

Simply put, I needed to stop paying cash and get a credit card; I transitioned from "layaway queen" to "cash queen".

"I do not care what you say, God said that's my car," I told the salesman and finance manager. I went home thinking nothing about it, the next day while at work, I made a call to check on the process and was told "we are working on it". When I returned to work, I received a call as I was about to leave for the day. Please hold for Lexington Grady, the caller said. "Ms. Baker, you said that God said that was your car," Mr. Grady said after the transfer. "So, when should I expect you to pick up God's and your car"? He went on to say, "We tried all of our secondary lenders, and they all said "No," but our last resort was the "main source" of "The Mercedes Benz Credit Corporation," and they said "Yes"!

It did not end there; I soon opened a clothing boutique, yes, I still knew how to grind and hustle to make money; but this time it was legal. There was no more looking over my shoulders for the "Poe Poe"—the police. I studied everything I could about starting a business in the fashion industry and marketing, I even assisted with the stripping, painting, and installation of the racks and equipment.

I had a "grand opening" that was smaller than that of a typical clothing store, but in a more intimate setting. In my boutique, I attracted customers who were looking for very specific styles and types of clothing. I stuck to my own styles, which pleased customers and they returned to my business. I developed relationships with my regular customers, whose requests and satisfaction aided the success of my boutique. I always gave them something to look forward to by displaying a "Bad purse, shoes or boot, and a piece of jewelry" accessory set. Someone always ended up with the entire set. Dorinda Clark

Cole of The Clark Sisters was one of my favorite clients; she autographed a photo to be displayed in the boutique with the words "You Keep Me Looking Good."

Learn how to start your own business and never underestimate your abilities. Remember that I did not have much as a child, I took the lack and shifted it in a way that kept me well-dressed while also bringing in another source of family income. My youngest son would always come into the boutique go straight to the register and say, "How much did we make today"? Yes, he served as my accountant, ensuring that my product and sales numbers were in sync.

Stop allowing your flesh to keep you from being who and want God desires for you to be! Never allow people and I mean, anyone, to tell you what you can or cannot be or do!

When God is prepared to do what He is going to do, that is, what He has predestined, it is done. When you give God what He desires, He will provide you with what you require. Leaders need more than empowerment, they need wisdom. *1 Kings 3:9 (KJV) "Give therefore thy servant an understanding heart to judge thy people, that I may discern between good and bad: for who is able to judge this thy so great a people". I* was endowed with the discernment to recognize the lack of wisdom and purity in today's leaders, those with other agendas and who are completely uninterested in the truth. I could see not only with my carnal eyes, but also through the spiritual lens.

Things in the spiritual realm began to change just as I was getting comfortable; I felt at ease in the church where I was, I progressed from choir member to praise and worship leader before becoming a church minister.

I was serving and I was held accountable. Nowadays, there is no accountability and many people go unnoticed. They have no formal education or training on how to divide God's word correctly; many are being licensed or ordained by those who lack true credentials whereas the Bible recommends that we must truly "know them that labor among you, and this knowing is spiritually. *1st Thessalonians 5 states, "Now, also we beseech you, brethren, get to know those who labor among you recognize them for what they are, acknowledge and appreciate and respect them."*

The subject of God-ordained authority is well-known to any Bible scholar who has thoroughly immersed themselves in the study of God's Word. God has been the orchestrator behind all earthly authority since the beginning; authority in the home, the nation, and (since Christ's time) the church. God established this to provide guidance and to maintain law and order.

Because man is born with a carnal nature, some of his choices tend to be contrary to God's holy will. So, what should church leaders do to earn the respect of their congregations? What should people do when Godly church leaders appear to be heading in the wrong direction?

Or, more specifically, what forms of church leadership and practical administration adhere to Biblical directives?

In this hour we truly need to be looking at the scriptural instructions that God has given to each of us regarding the issues relating to those who have been placed over us in spiritual authority. We have church leaders that have truly gone wild, the church has gone insane! Anything goes without an explanation or an excuse; Compromise has made its way into the church.

The church is so title-driven, arrogant, and pumped up! I've never seen so much flesh on display in my life, from the leadership! Because of the fleshly display in so many ways, you cannot hear or receive any words.

1 Timothy 2:9 KJV, "In the same way, women should dress modestly, with shamefacedness and sobriety, rather than with braided hair or gold. This is in the Bible! You must first free yourself before you can help someone else.

The ability to develop and maintain healthy ongoing relationships, with integrity, has become a challenge for many. Do as I say, not as I do kind of leadership. Doing the opposite of what the word of God says and causing the sheep to go astray and leave the church.

Some are challenging the Bible, the Word of God; some are disobeying the word of God, doing their own thing, and saying, and "Who's going to check me"? Good is now evil and evil is now good and acceptable. The church is acting, looking and sounding like that of the world. Where is the holiness? *Leviticus 19:20, "Be Holy for I Am Holy"*

It is very sad that as leaders in the church, we preach, pray, dance, shout, speak in tongues, prophesy, and lay hands; but at the end of the service, it is difficult for one to be followed out and not be caught in a sinful act. The exposure of church leaders within the news media has been great. I understand that no one is perfect, however, the Bible say in *2 Corinthians 6:17 KJV, "Wherefore come out from among them, and be ye separate, saith the Lord, and touch not the unclean thing; and I will receive you."* The Holy Spirit is a keeper if you want to be kept! However, you are playing with fire if you go the way of disobedience, and the consequence of disobedience is eternal damnation. In *2 Chronicles 7:14 KJV, it says," If my people, which are called by my name, shall humble themselves, and pray, and seek my face, and turn their wicked ways:then will I hear from heaven, and will forgive their sin, and will heal their land."*

The Lord woke me up one Sunday morning and told me to get dressed because I had an assignment, but I didn't. My phone soon rang with the person asking if I had an assignment and I responded "No". "You have an assignment now, God said you have a word for us," he replied. I called my assistant, quickly dressed, gathered my belongings, and left. While ministering, I heard the Lord say to tell my people, "The Day and Hour will come when we all shall stand before Me, but will you be able to stand before Me, Naked and Unashamed"? There will be "No Fig Leaves!" The bishop and other church leaders jumped to their feet shouting, "Oh God, My God!"

If you are a church leader reading this book, remember that warning comes before destruction! The Lord sent warning before His wrath everywhere in the Bible! Come out of your sin, what God says is more important than what man thinks. You can look north, south, east, and west, but don't forget to look up, He sees and knows everything. Some people are in ministry for the wrong reasons, and winning souls is not one of them for them, it is not about the "Call, Charge, or Mandate"; instead, their eyes are focused on the spotlight, the title, and the lifestyle, a large church congregation and the offerings. Indeed, many are Called, but only a few are Chosen.

Please allow me to pause for a moment. Over the years, I had to learn that I was not meant to be a part or member of a church, but of the "Body of Christ; of God's Kingdom". "The Lord's Prayer" is well-known in the Bible, but how many people who repeat it understand what they are praying?

This prayer, known as the "Lord's Prayer," was given in response to a request from one of Jesus' disciples. *"Now it came to pass, that one of His disciples said to Him, Lord, teach us to pray as John taught his disciples." (Luke 11:1).* The entire prayer is important, but how many people truly understand what they are praying when they say, *"Thy Kingdom Come" (Matthew 6:10; Luke 11:2, KJV)*? What exactly is this Kingdom, and when will it arrive? Some believe the kingdom has already been established in their hearts; others believe it is the church, while others believe it is heaven. It isn't any of these, according to the Bible!

Many of Jesus' parables were about the "Kingdom of God", either directly stated (Mark 4:26-32; Luke 13:20-21) or clearly implied (Luke 14:15–24). Jesus' audience realized that His message was about a coming kingdom (Luke 19:11–27). They misinterpreted the timing, but they understood that He taught about a coming Kingdom. From the beginning, Jesus' message was about the Kingdom of God (Mark 1:14–15).

Kings reign and rule in a Kingdom; this is where they exercise their authority and ownership rights. One must first understand both who they are and to whom they belong. God's Kingdom is within you, and His desire is for His Kingdom to be manifested through and in us. But we must respect His wishes; we must die to the flesh on a daily basis, which we despise. It has to be his will and way for anything that is not a part of God's Kingdom will not last.

Jesus is the Almighty and Kingdom people must realize that they are created first and foremost by and for God. They must have the mind of Christ and grow into Him daily by daily beholding Him through His Word.

Jesus is calling individuals, who do not follow the flow of the world's system, but who step out of their comfort zones and do the works of God in faith; these are the chosen few who act on their knowledge. Note this sober warning: "Enter by the narrow gate; for wide is the gate and broad is the way that leads to destruction, and there are many who go in by it. *Because narrow is the gate and difficult is the way which leads to life, and there are few who find it" (Matthew 7:13–14).*

Every true believer should strive for God's rule on Earth. *"But seek first the kingdom of God and His righteousness, and all these things shall be added to you," Christ said (Matthew 6:33).* Everyone who prioritizes this goal in their minds and hearts will pray every day for what Jesus said we should pray for: Thy Kingdom Come! We must become Kingdom minded as being church minded is insufficient.

Church folk can be the worst. As a church leader, I've been lied on, discussed and more. There was a time when I was even removed from my position as a worship leader due to the lies of other church leaders.

But you must be reborn and be able to remove the hurt, pain, and memory from yourself. I continued to attend Sunday and weekly services, even though everyone was wondering why I was not doing what the Shepherd had assigned me to do. Yes, I was humiliated, but God required that I sit face to face with the same church members and bear it all. I had to learn that my situation is never my conclusion, and they had no idea that I had accepted the assignment. I was never one to relinquish my power, authority, or control easily; once again, you must know "Who You Are and Whose You Are". What they did not realize was that I was driven.

"LIFE WITH PURPOSE"

The Lord told me to go to school after I accepted the call to be chosen. Now, let me tell you that I went to school for other things, and now I must go back. I began to ask the Lord why I needed this, what it was for; His response was that as a female minister, I could never be denied by man because I would be anointed, educated, and know how to divide the Word of God correctly. I was born into this life of destiny and purpose.

But first, let me tell you about one of my most memorable moments in ministry. I frequently struggled with telling people what The Lord had given me to tell them, especially after I released a word that The Lord had told me would be rejected but would come to pass. Her name was Linda, and I released a word that she from the very start rejected and said "No I am already going through something, and I know that God is not going to add to it, but what she did not know was that I also wasn't continuously say that this wasn't something I asked for.

"I don't receive that," she said, and I replied that I was only a messenger. "See, I told you I did not want to tell her that," I said as I walked away. Well, I received an apology and was told "God, the Lord is truly using you". She told me what was going on and that it was exactly what the Lord had told me to release to her. Let me pause here to emphasize how important the timing of God is. It strengthens our faith by forcing us to wait and trust in God. It ensures that He and He alone, receive the glory and praise for bringing us through." *Psalms 31:15 says, "My times are in Your Hands".* At the right time, God will provide your need.

He Is Patient as shown in 2 Peter 3:8-9, "But do not forget this one thing, dear friends, with the Lord a day is like a thousand years, and a thousand years are like a day. The Lord is not slow in keeping his promise, as some understand slowness. All Glory to GOD for every word that was spoken, manifested, and came to pass. Every detail of the instructions given by the Lord was as clear as the day they were given. But I would always say "Lord all of You and none of me, I die to self and flesh". She frequently tells me that she writes down her prophecies and dates them, and that if I speak to them, she knows they are from the mouth of GOD.

Let me state unequivocally that a prophet is and will be held accountable for every word spoken as a spokesman/mouthpiece of GOD. As a prophet, you must keep your ears to God's mouth. You must have clean ears and guard your gates. Not allowing anything and everything into your spirit. Some things are meant to be received rather than said or released because everything has a time, season, and purpose. There is a season for everything, and a time for everything under heaven.

The Bible in *Ecclesiastes 3:1-8* says; *"A time to be born, and a time to die; a time to plant, and a time to pluck up that which is planted; A time to kill, and a time to heal; a time to break down, and a time to build up; A time to weep, and a time to laugh; a time to mourn, and a time to dance; A time to cast away stones, and a time to gather stones together; a time to embrace, and a time to refrain from embracing; A time to get, and a time to lose; a time to keep, and a time to cast away; A time to rend, and a time to sow; a time to keep silence, and a time to speak; A time to love, and a time to hate; a time of war, and a time of peace."*

Remember the three words of Prophecy: Time, Turn, and Season; and that everything is conditional. Be patient and wait on the Lord, aswell as on directions. *"In their hearts, humans plan their course, but theLord establishes their steps," says Proverbs 16:9.* Never go out on yourown timing, do not try to get ahead of God and never go anywhere without directions or instructions. You should only be afraid of yourself, yes, you must die to your flesh; otherwise, it will destroy you. Now, that spoken word will necessitate some effort on your part to ensure that you are first in alignment with the word of GOD.

Second, faithfully carry out your instructions. You must understand and trust GOD's timing, wait for God, the Lord! One thing I am certain of is the discernment of GOD's timing. God's ways are perfect (Psalm 18:30). As a result, His timing is impeccable; He is never early, and He is never late. Because of our natural human impatience, we may not wantto put up with or wait for something or someone at times. Learn to be patient

and to please wait on the Lord!

The General Overseer-The Apostle

While serving as a church leader, my ministering assignments increased, and I was traveling, preaching the gospel and prophesying God's Word to God's people. During a church event, I was assigned a task; I was and still am the type to tell people to let me pray about it before I respond. I was asked several times before finally saying yes. It was a church women's conference, and my role would be to attend to all of the female ministers who would come to the church to minister during the conference.

I was to be their attendant and security all in one because I was a Sworn Law Enforcement Officer. I agreed to do something I did not want to do, but little did I know that I would meet some of the most powerful and influential women in ministry and the world.

One such woman was Dr. Barbara King, one of Atlanta's most historic ministers and the founder of the Hillside Chapel and Truth Center, Inc. in Atlanta, Georgia. For many years, Reverend Dr. Barbara Lewis King played an important role in the African American church and community.

Apostle Dr. Vanessia M. Livingston was one of the women of God I had to drive to the hotel from the airport. I was told she was an older woman with a pacemaker, so I assumed she would be someone I would have to help with everything, but to my surprise, she was nothing like what I expected. This General stepped off the plane and spoke into almost every aspect of my life. She told me she was there to minister, but

God had not only told her; He had also shown her a woman He was sending her to assist.

This Woman of God was in town for five days, and I was being poured into at her feet. She answered every question, and she shared details from her life story that helped me understand not just who I was, but of Whom I was. She dove into God's purpose and plan for my life, but she never forgot to tell me that it all came at a cost; a cost that others could not or would not be able to bear; and that the warfare would be fierce.

She confirmed that what I was experiencing was spiritual warfare and that I needed to be aware of demon power. She showed me how to recognize (you must know how to recognize demons). She showed me how to prepare and battle in spiritual warfare. She educated me on the true weapons of warfare. Mother taught me that if I did the fisty cuffty battle, fighting in the physical, I would never win. She taught me about earthly thinking and that my obedience would be paramount in my reaching and completing my kingdom assignment". I was taught about God's given power, authority, and the charge placed on my life.

The most important lesson she taught me was about

forgiveness and love. She taught me how to move past the pain and even love the hell out of those who had hurt or harmed me. She had to assist me in letting go of everything I had to let go of and this had to be done for me to fulfill God's plan and purpose for my life.

Let me tell you, this woman touched on every emotion I was feeling or facing: the rejection spirit, the death spirit; when my father had passed away, I was not told until two days after his death. The spirit of heaviness caused by the attacks on my mother that I had witnessed, jealousy; all of which had a stronghold on me were shattered, and I was freed from them all. We talked and prayed about what was at the root of it all. The time we spent together taught me that I needed to know the size of my God first and foremost, to know the size of my gift. To truly understand that I did not have a gift, but that I was the gift. We discussed the secret place where I found peace and exchanged with the Father, the Son, and the Holy Spirit. She became my spiritual checker, the one who would call me up and expose my sins and shortcomings.

If I may inquire, who is your checker? Who is teaching you about holiness and accountability? Who is holding you accountable? Accountability is essential for the functioning of any society, and Christian accountability is no exception. Christians require support and comfort, which they frequently find through Christian accountability. Accountability requires two things: trust and the ability to relate. There must be trusted to establish Christian accountability. Trust is a slow process that takes time to develop and grow. As people gather to share, they begin to establish a rapport with one another. Accountability entails being willing to open and share sensitive or personal information. Therefore, trust is essential. When you sense trust, you are more willing to share your deepest thoughts without fear. Relating is an important factor in Christian accountability.

The Bible emphasizes the importance of strong accountability among believers; every believer needs at least one other person to confide in, pray with, listen to, and encourage them. The Bible speaks of Christian accountability. We see first that God holds us accountable; *Romans 14:12 says, "So then each of us shall give account of himself to God", this is personal accountability. Christian accountability is encouraging each other to grow into spiritual maturity. Hebrews 10:24 says, "And let us consider how we may spur one another on toward love and good deeds." 1st Thessalonians 5:11 says to encourage one another and build each other up.*

So, are you accountable to someone? Do you have a friend to whom you can go? Will that person hold you accountable in your spiritual walk? Are you the type of person that people can come to when they need accountability?

The Attack on My Children: The Counterattack of Satan

When the devil knows that he has lost you, he will launch out an all-out attack on your life. After all, that I had just experienced with the woman of God, he decided to come after me. However, when the devil sees the "Job or Jobette" inside of you, he then places his focus on those closest, near and dear to you.

When the devil attacked one of my children, it was once again one of the most critical times in my life. When the devil comes after you and cannot stop you, he attacks those closest to you. Attacking my children and parents is the worst thing anyone can do. Isa. 54:17 "No weapon formed against thee shall prosper, and every tongue that rises against thee in judgment thou shalt condemn. This is the inheritance of the LORD's servants, and their righteousness is of me, says the LORD.

This was a time when my faith was truly put to the test, and warfare was raging in my life from all sides. It came from my job, church, close friends, and, of course, satan's attack on my house. According to the Bible, our weapons of warfare are not carnal, but rather mighty through the destruction of strongholds (2 Corinthians 10:4).

I've always been the type to avoid battles unless they were forced upon me, especially if they were physical. I knew I was in for spiritual encounters with both familiar and unfamiliar spirits and demons.

I was well trained and ready to go into spiritual warfare. I knew my effective areas of warfare and was taught to recognize the patterns of my enemy's attacks. Listen, some of you really need to calm down, stop rebuking God and His assigned angels, and learn to hear God clearly. God cannot speak to you because you are afraid. I was taught the tools of the trade, how to fight, and how to hear God's voice and wait for his instructions. I do not want to spend too much time on this because it would necessitate another book on another level, but if you are going into battle, please know and recognize the demonic spirit you are going up against. As a little note there are prerequisites you must possess before entering the battles of spiritual warfare.

Satan sent his imps to attack my eldest brother, who was

paralyzed from the waist down. I was about eight years old at the time of his traffic accident. I got a call that he had been burned and was being flown to The Shane Burn Center in Gainesville, Florida.

The trip was a road trip, and I had a business to run as well as other responsibilities, but The Lord told me to go there on assignment. The devil did his job by attempting to derail me, but God! I had a flat tire! I dialed 911 and informed the operator of my predicament as well as my public safety affiliation. I soon had the help of a local Deputy Sheriff, who removed the entire luggage and changed the tire then sent me off with the words of prayer and well wishes. I arrived at the hospital but was met with "Sorry, you cannot see him"! I again told the staff there who I was, that I was family and I had driven from Atlanta for hours to get there.

I was allowed into the facility to see my brother. He was in bad shape, and it was said that the next 24 to 48 hours (about 2 days) would be extremely crucial to his living or passing away as he was burned with 2nd and 3rd degree burns to his upper torso. I quickly said aloud "He shall live and not die!" They informed me that the swelling and the fluids would become worst, again I said "No, I Believe God." I dressed into the required safety attire for my visitation, and I went in to see my brother lying there all bandaged up with tubes running from everywhere.

I laid my hands upon my brother's leg, and I began to pray. I began to speak, decree and declare life and his healing; the monitor began to make some sounds and the staff came running, but I spoke in and with the authority of God that he is fine; that the Hand of God was moving. I continued and completed my prayer and the monitors returned to nor- mal. Again, I said aloud, "He shall live and not die"; the attending nurses looked at me strangely as I then proceeded to point my hands towards the rooms where I could see other patients lying in the beds and I prayed and spoke words of life.

At that time the Lord said to me that 3 of the patients there would not make it, that he was releasing them from their pain and calling them home. I spoke briefly with a nurse about my brother and before leaving I shared with her what the Lord had shared about the other burn patients. She looked at me with disbelief. As I was leaving, I was approached by a woman who asked me if I would pray a prayer for someone in one of the other rooms; my response was "The Lord shall heal them."

The next day the visit was delayed due to my brother's bandages having to be changed and it would take some time.

The wounds would have to be cleaned, medicated creams reapplied, and fresh bandages applied. I knew this would be painful and he would be in tremendous pain. I knew because I had been burned by boiling hot water as a child. I waited patiently to see him and when it was time, I entered the room, dressed up. As I approached my brother, I could physically see with my eyes that his body, that is, the blotting and swelling were going down before my eyes.

Yes, I mean right before my eyes and the staff's words were "We don't understand". Normally the patient's condition became worse, but my brother's condition shifted and turned for the better. But God! I saw the same nurse looking at me again in disbelief. Upon leaving, she shared with me that the patients in the three rooms had indeed passed away, and the patient's family member that had asked me to pray was now responding.

The next day I was expecting to see my brother in the room where he had been, but God had yet again moved, and my brother was moved into rehabilitation.

Again, the doctors and staff were in disbelief and did not understand how he was admitted in grave condition but was healing and recovering in such a manner that was medically unrealistic! Oh, I feel Jesus right there! But GOD!

Master's in Leadership; M.Div.

The Next move of my life was to return to school again and upon graduating, I received a dual Master's in Leadership and Divinity and I again graduated at the top of my class. The Lord spoke to me that I needed to be well equipped for my journey; it was not easy as I experienced attacks there as well. It may seem strange to hear that I experienced attack in a Bible College but satan does not care where he attacks, his aim and goal is to kill, steal and destroy the vision and plan for your life; you have a date with destiny and his plan is to stop you by any means.

Saints, Aint's and the Others

In 2008, I ran into a former member of a church where we had both been members. During my membership, I had no personal contact with this individual. This individual was discovered to be extremely manipulative, deceitful, and cunning. She and a very respectable person duped and conned Christians out of large sums of money. Allow me to pause it right here and say that you need the gift of discernment to recognize wolves in sheep's clothing/garments.

To understand or know something through the power of the Holy Spirit is what spiritual discernment means. It includes perceiving the true character of people and the source and meaning of spiritual manifestations. "The one right use of judgment is how you feel," Jesus says in a course on miracles. When I finally allowed myself to feel my emotions, it turned into a torrent of tears.

Everything that appears to be God is not always what it appears to be. According to the Bible, gifts are given without repentance; *Romans 11:29 says, "For the gifts and calling of God are without repentance."*

God will not change His mind about what He has called you to do if you do not repent. If God has called you, whether you have obeyed or not, that calling remains and if God gave you a gift along a certain line, that gift remains.

The gift refers to the fivefold ministry gifts: Apostle, Prophet, Evangelist, Pastor, and Teacher. You may or may not be called to the fivefold ministry. But everyone can be involved in the ministry of helps, which is necessary and very important part of the Body of Christ. And in one sense of the word, we are all called to preach.

A person may not be faithful to God's call on his or her life, but the call remains; God doesn't go back on the call. So, let us all obey God and respond to the call by living a fully holy life. I am not the one to pass judgment on anyone because we will all stand before God in judgment one day, but this man used his street smarts and God-given gift to manipulate women in the church. When I tell you that both had strong ungodly ways and told lies; yes, they lied to get what they wanted, and he even preached about himself and what he did to these women to instill fear in them.

It is tragic that greed, selfishness, and a love of money can overpower such a divine vessel. The Bible according to *1st Timothy 6:10 "For the love of money is the root of all evil: which while some coveted after, they have erred from the faith, and pierced themselves through with many sorrows"*. The love of money is condemned as a sin in Christianity, primarily through texts such as Ecclesiastes 5:10 and 1 Timothy 6:10. Rather than money itself, the Christian condemnation is directed at avarice and greed. In the Christian classification of sins, avarice is one of the seven deadly sins.

My trust in these two people cost me my home, my place

of residence, and much more. I ended up living out of my car and going to that person I thought was my friend's house for a couple of nights to an extended stay. I discovered that these two were wolves disguised as sheep. One in the pulpit at least 300 days a year (about 10 months) preaching, praying, and yes, prophesying to the people, but living a life of taking and stealing from God's people. They brought their street knowledge into the pulpit in order to scheme and defraud God's people.

The others attempted to destroy me. She attempted to destroy my name, character, and everything I touched. But I had to accept that she was truly sick when she fantasized and lied about being married to a man she had never married, even though she was married to her own husband; every lie was covered up by this God-fearing man. Let me remind you that these are "church folk," with one of them being a major leader of the gospel scamming and scheming God's people. I often wondered, if they heard God call them into ministry, why didn't they hear Him call them out of sin?

This woman killed off her own mother by claiming that she died of cancer. She later told me that she went to get her hair done and came home to find her father dead in her bed. Soon after, I learned that her brother had been killed during an attempted robbery at the barber shop he owned. After speaking with a friend, I learned that she had told them that both of her parents had died in a car accident with an 18-wheeler truck, only to discover that her parents and brother were still alive.

I started to recognize them for who they truly were. God will sometimes create an illusion for your enemies to reveal themselves. I was both hurt and angry, and I wanted revenge, yes, revenge. I had to do some serious praying and let me say this: never mistake someone's kindness for weakness, because not all kindness is weakness. All females are not weak or afraid, and they may just come after you. Let me help you; the things I know and have learned about God, Jesus, and the church, my mother and the mothers of Zion and the church, taught me but the streets taught me about the world.

Let's just say that, as you can see, I've been around a few blocks and don't fear flesh-man. Some people will go to any length to lay you down and ensure that you stay that way! The gift of discernment is something you should ask God for because you need it. It will assist you in seeing slap through some people and may keep you out of jail and prison. Things happened during that season of my life that broke my heart and opened my eyes and mind even more to the ways of God and the ways of man. But it was God's Grace that kept me going.

For a while, I got into my flesh, and the old fleshly me rose. Let's just say I had a residue of unhealed hurts and unresolved issues. A hurting person can be extremely dangerous and deadly. But, if you have an ear to hear God's voice, then get out of your emotions and govern your mind. I had to pray nonstop every day, and I remembered that the Bible also says, *"Dearly beloved, avenge not yourselves, but rather give place unto wrath: for it is written, Vengeance is mine; I will repay, saith the Lord." Romans 12:19*. I heard the Voice of the Lord saying, "What you might do he may recover, that which I shall do if I say that there is no recovery, he shall not recover."

2 Timothy 3:1–17 "But keep in mind that there will be times of difficulty in the last days. People will be lovers of self, lovers of money, proud, arrogant, abusive, disobedient to their parents, ungrateful, unholy, heartless, unappeasable, slanderous, without self-control, brutal, not loving good, treacherous, reckless, swollen with conceit, lovers of pleasure rather than lovers of God, appearing to be godly but denying its power. Stay away from such people ".

"Whoever loves money never has enough; whoever loves wealth is never satisfied with their income. Wealth is worthless in the day of wrath, but righteousness delivers from death." Proverbs 11:28. *"He who trusts in his riches will fall, but the righteous shall flourish as the green leaf."*

Lastly, let us see what the Bible says about righting wrongs; "And he shall make full restitution for his wrong, adding a fifth to it and giving it to him. So, to the two people who hurt me so badly, that is your warning, I pray that God will have mercy on you. Oh, I Feel Jesus Right There!

To right a wrong, you must be willing to face the Almighty God's consequences! The day and hour are coming when we will all stand before God; the question is, will you be able to stand naked and unashamed before Him, with every wrong made right? There will be no fig leaves! There will be nowhere to hide or run.

Let me tell you that my "flesh" and "faith" were put to the ultimate test. I had to remember what I had read in the Word of God, that what-ever is on the inside of you will manifest on the outside. That word had to be applied to my own test; *"And beside this, giving all diligence, add to your faith virtue; and to virtue knowledge; and to knowledge temperance; and to* temperance patience;

and to patience godliness; and to godliness brotherly kindness; and to brotherly kindness charity (2 Peter 1:5- 7 KJV). I could not let the devil win; *"Neither give place to the devil" Ephesians 4:27 KJV.* I placed it in the Master's Hands, but not before my assistant had to talk me out of taking matters into my own hands. A quick word to the wise; women are powerful and dangerous.

Listen, forget what or who may have hurt you, but never forget the lesson it taught you. Separate and release people that are pulling, tearing, and holding you down. Some people, relationships and associations are just toxic; break every ungodly soul tie and ask the Lord to perform a spiritual detox.

Psalm 37:3 says, "Trust in the LORD and do good; dwell in the land and enjoy safe pasture. Delight yourself in the LORD and he will give you the desires of your heart".

I needed help handling this trial and God already knew what and who I needed; He placed me in the path of yet another Mother of Zion: Mother Judy Hines.

Mother Judy Hines was no joke. People say that this Woman of God would pull whatever the Lord placed within you out. To begin with, I was fasting the entire time I was in her house. For those of you that do not know what it means to fast, fasting is to "abstain from all or some kinds of food or drink, television, social media, shopping and more especially as a religious observance.

Fasting is a deliberate abstinence from physical gratification, usually going without food for a period to achieve a greater spiritual goal. Fasting is intentionally denying the flesh in order to gain a response from the spirit. When fasting, you say "No" to yourself, your flesh and "Yes" to God.

Matthew 6:16, where Jesus is teaching His disciples basic principles of godly living, is one of the most telling passages in the Bible in which fasting is mentioned. When He speaks about fasting, He says, "When you fast," not "If you fast"; Jesus' words imply that fasting will be a regular practice in the lives of His followers, and fasting is a significant and normal part of my life. I stayed before the Lord in prayers, while fasting and if Mother Judy did not hear me praying; she would let me know by saying "I can't hear you praying".

The Scripture says, "Let your reasonableness be known to everyone. The Lord is at hand; do not be anxious about anything, but in everything by prayer and supplication with thanksgiving let your requests be made known to God. And the peace of God, which surpasses all understanding, will guard your hearts and your minds in Christ Jesus." Prayer is not just about asking God for things you need or desire. It is about establishing a relationship with Him built on faith and trust in Him. God knows the desires of your heart long before you even think to ask, but he still loves to hear from us whether you are asking for guidance or giving thanks because it draws you closer to him.

But the Bible also says to pray without cease, that is, to pray always. *1st Thessalonians 5:16-18 "Rejoice always, pray without ceasing, and give thanks in all circumstances; for this is the will of God in Christ Jesus for you"*. I need to stop right there because I am about to get caught up on prayer, so let us continue this journey.

When I exited the room, I would have to make sure I was properly dressed before proceeding ahead of her. Upon getting into her presence the first thing I heard would be "What is God saying, what is the word from the Lord". Okay, let's pause here to clarify two words: "Prophet andProphetic".

First, a Prophet or Prophetess, respectively male and female, is some-one who delivers messages from God. They are those who speak divinely inspired revelations, have more than ordinary spiritual and moral insight, and can predict future events. They are commonly called spiritual seers. A prophet is someone who receives supernatural revelation and speaks in the name of God. Naturally, he or she is frequently used in the spiritual gift of prophecy, as well as the revelation gifts of the word of wisdom, the word of knowledge, and the discernment of spirits.

Let me make it clear that not everyone that speaks prophetically is a prophet. Some may operate and walk in the office of a prophet, while others may have the gift bestowed upon them to prophesy.

A Prophet's primary function in the Old Testament was to serve as God's representative or ambassador by communicating God's word to his people. True prophets never spoke on their own authority or shared their personal opinions, but rather delivered the message God Himself gave them. Several texts make this explicit. God promised Moses, "Now go; I will help you speak and will teach you what to say" (Exod. 4:12). God assured Moses, "I will raise up for [my people] a prophet like you and I will put my words in his mouth. He will tell them everything I command him" (Deut. 18:18). The Lord said to Jeremiah, "I have put my words in your mouth" (Jer 1:9). God commissioned Ezekiel by saying, "You must speak my words to them" (Ezek. 2:7).

Any believer may be used of God in the gift of prophecy as the Spirit wills, but that does not make him or her, a prophet. A prophet is, first, a minister who can preach or teach with an anointing. The prophet is the second highest calling (see the order as it is listed in 1 Cor. 12:28). True prophets would bring a revelation of God's displeasure of their disobedience.

The Gift vs The Office

The gift is for all but being called to the ministry as a prophet of God (or into the office of a prophet) is not for all. The office of a prophet is very different from operating in the gift of prophecy. As a calling, it is firstly affirmed by God to that individual, and then at a later stage, it's affirmed by man, specifically by other members of the five-fold ministry. Most probably this affirmation will come by another prophet, but it can be confirmed by one of the other offices too (apostle, teacher, pastor and evangelist). Just because a man or a woman is called into the office of a prophet, does not mean they are ready to be behind a pulpit or put into a place of influence.

Office of a Prophet/Prophetess

- It is a gift from the Godhead

- God chooses the office; it's not our choice. I was born into It

- It is to train, equip, direct, correct, warn and govern

- He/she is a gift to the Body of Christ

- He/she is part of the five-fold ministry to equip the saints

- The calling is for life

Gift of Prophecy

In 1 Corinthians 14, Paul encourages everyone to pursue the gift of prophecy (v. 1). The primary purpose of prophetic ministry is to strengthen, encourage, and comfort believers (v. 3). In other words, "The one who prophesies edifies the church" (v. 4). Prophecy may also bring conviction of sin to unbelievers who happen to be visiting the gathering of God's people, as the secrets of their hearts are laid bare (vs. 24–25).

Lastly, I cannot say this strongly enough; "Not everyone is a true prophet" and please remember that gifts are given without repentance (Romans 11:29). Let me give you a little help here by mentioning some characteristics that would help you identify a false prophet.

Characteristics of a False Prophet:

- It is all about them!

- They are not under the spiritual authority of a senior pastor/leader. In other words, there is no accountability, as they think they know all things.

- They bring dissention quickly within the leadership team and then in other areas of the church body. There is always controversy or strife associated with them.

- They are judgmental, critical, and use manipulation to get what they want. They are not seeing or speaking through the heart and eyes of Father God but speaking through the wrong spirit of condemnation.

- They may have been correct and true in the beginning, but due to offenses they have received, they now operate out of anger, frustration, and hurt.

In these days some young women would not want or feel the need for someone to pour into them, they would look at this as abuse, someone that was crazy; or they would say "It doesn't take all of that". If you know what I now know, you'll agree that it takes all of that and more. These are new days and a new era, but God remains the same; yesterday, today, and forever.

Mother Judy understood who I was in the Kingdom and what it would take to get me where I needed to go. I could not eat but I had to cook for others; I couldn't wear certain things or colors; I had to stay in the presence of God again and again; this time with the woman of God who taught me many things about God. "Watch and pray," the Bible says, and I truly understand how to pray and recognize a divine move. I learned to protect my ear gates and to discern the spirits I encountered. I learned that no matter what, God's timing is everything; you can never rush God.

I knew I had met and crossed paths with her for a reason. God had a plan and a purpose for everything. People come into your life for a reason, some sent by God, some by Satan to cause havoc, and some to bless and curse you. But God had me on a mission to learn everything I could from every sold-out mother in Zion to help me get to my destiny. I learned at a young age to listen to the elders who had lived longer and had a story to tell in order to capture some wisdom and share the knowledge.

I was taught to be a lifelong learner and that knowledge is power. When I left this woman's feet I left with a greater level of power, wisdom, and hunger for God; I left with a thirst like never before.

JUDAH DOVE

During all of this, I was riding with the Lord one day when he spoke to me and gave me the name "Judah Dove". He said, "Write the vision, make it plain, and go forth in the vineyard." There is an assignment for those who have been raped, molested, or sexually exploited in the vineyard. "Your assignment is to ensure that healing, restoration, and deliverance occur in their lives so that they may be of use for the Kingdom." Life with a purpose", was the word he gave to me. He made me sit down and write my first of many Business Plans.

This plan would be used to apply for my 501 C3, which I would acquire in 30 days (about 4 and a half weeks), even after being told that it could take up to a year. When God has a plan for your life, he will open doors, and when He gives a vision, He provides provision. Nothing and no one can stop God's Hands or move; the greater the battle, the greater the move of God and He was constantly moving in my life.

I worked from home for a while, but I had a strong desire to have a group home for the survivors. We had a visitor at our table while dining at a restaurant with my then-right hand and board member Jerri Flood. The visitor was a man who sat at the table behind us and stated that he had overheard our discussion about the need for a building; he gave me a business card and told me to call him. The waitress informed us as we prepared to leave that the same gentleman had covered the cost of our food. We left a tip and said our goodbyes before leaving the restaurant. I called the gentleman the next morning and was told that he had a building that I could use totally free and that all I needed to do was present him with the proper information for my 501 C3.

I wept and danced right there. I mean, I got my praise on, I yelled at the top of my lungs, "Glory! God be praised"! The contract was delivered, signed, and notarized within a few days. This man was a stranger, but he was a Christian looking to bless someone. He over heard our conversation and took action to bless rape, molestation, and exploitation survivors. He insisted on being a part of the vision. And it did not end there, as time passed, we needed an office and I prayed and gave it over to the Lord. I discussed the need for an office with my then-assistant.

She asked a friend who worked as a real estate agent for help in finding a building; her friend quickly responded that she wanted me to look at a building. We met with the agent at the location, while waiting for the owner; I began to pray and the Lord said, "This is your office". When the owner arrived, he opened the doors to the building and gave us a thorough tour. I was so impressed with the structure because it had everything I needed.

First, there was a furnished lobby and boardroom for board meetings, as well as a small kitchen with a microwave, refrigerator, and coffee and tea maker. There was a room for intake, a counseling room, and, of course, an office for me, the CEO, with a cherry wood desk. I started telling myself, "This is my building!" I spoke with the owner about the building's need and his desire to learn more about the organization-Judah Dove. He told me about his ideas and wanted to know how he could start a non-profit organization.

Listen, to cut a long story short, this man was a Christian! We chatted for a couple of minutes, but during all of us leaving the building I shared with my assistant that God was going to show me favor concerning the building.

I told her that was our building and that she should follow up with the owner about it. Well, about three days, I was on the south side when I received a call from my assistant asking, "Where are you?" I told her I was on my way home from the south side and asked her what was going on. "Well, you said God would bless you with the building and that the building was ours." "Yes, that is our building," I replied. "I just spoke with the owner, and the building is yours for free!" I was at a traffic light on Camp Creek Parkway in South Atlanta; I jumped out of the car, screaming "Glory! Thank You Jesus".

I ran around the car, dancing, and then jumped back in before the light changed! People were honking and saying, "You better bless and praise Him," and they had no idea what the Lord had just done for me. She was shouting my name, unaware that I had jumped out of the car, dancing and praising. "You doubted my words," I told her, and she said "Yes, but all I can say is my God!" When the Lord gives you a vision and tells you to do something, trust and obey," I told her. When

God gives you a vision, He will make provisions, open doors, and keep His word. I needed much more than I had, but all I needed was God's favor and it was working in my favor. Sometimes you do not need to have money, when favor is all you need.

Mother Dr. Gertrude Stacks

I learned about this great general after attending a service led by Mother in Zion, Dr. Estella Boyd; this was a long time ago. It was such an experience I will never forget, one that would make you want to flee, but which I found myself drawn to instead. I got my first shot into the spirit realm there and ended up in many of her services, followed by up close and personal encounters; the numerous times I received impartations (the shots, the charges), the oil that was given to me for personal and ministry use, the teachings, the wise words. The wealth of knowledge that she shared was invaluable. Her prophecies were accurate and on point every time and her gift of discerning of spirits, let's just say you could not hide. If you went to a service and desired deliverance or healing, it was in the room; and believe me, you left that service healed, set free, and delivered. There would be a Shift into another place if you were in any service.

Death of My Brother

When you think things cannot get any worse, especially when you see God's hand moving on your behalf; my life appeared to be going well and then my oldest sibling died, the same brother who had been severely burned years before a retired military officer and long-haul truck driver. He was the first of eight children, and my mother was 93 years old, which was a major concern for me. I am the youngest of my siblings and my mother's baby; I sat with my mother during my brother's service and as I wiped her tears, the Lord said to me to "Watch and pray". God is mindful of your tears.

My brother's death shattered my mother's heart; he had read the Bible to her every day. After the ceremony, I made it a duty to call and pray with my mother, as well as speak over her. I felt the need to stay with my mother for a while, but I was told that I needed to return to Atlanta because I was one of the honorees. The United Churches of God in Christ honored me with the Citizen of Valor Award for my community service and

Judah Dove's works and services for survivors of rape, molestation and exploitation.

God was showing me that my life and works were not in vain. "May the works I have done speak for me," says an old song. God told me that everything I had been through and would continue to go through was not for me, but for someone else. I would be my own witness and testifier. My witness, preaching, and teaching the gospel grew stronger by the day, and it seemed that the Lord was using me to minister and witness to His people everywhere I went: the gas station, the grocery store and even the post office.

The Lord will put your faith to the test. We always need Him to do things in our lives, but to whom much is given, much is expected; are you capable of meeting God's expectations? Life with a Purpose, do you know what God's plan for your life is? Some people, I've noticed, appear to want to forget or even hide from their past; they are unwilling to share their life's journey in terms of what the Lord has healed, set free, and delivered them from. Everything I've gone through has been at the hands of God; I have a God-given testimony of my transformation from a "Pit Queendom" to a "King's Palace", I am now a "True Queendom", and no longer a "Diva".

Passing of My Mother, My Queen

As previously stated, my mother was my queen, and I was her baby. I sent my mother chocolate-covered strawberries and fruit for Valentine's, Easter, and Mother's Day every year, and she loved them. But for the lastten years, we'd gathered in Florida to celebrate her with banquets, beach days, cookouts, banquets, and so much more. My mother became ill, and the nurse told me to come right away; this is where I run out of things to say. My mother had a lot of life left in her, but she was broken-hearted because of my brother's death. No mother would want to bury a child in their 90s. I know she was thinking that he should have been the one laying her to rest and not otherwise. It was a terrible experience for me; the death of my queen shook the core of me, the very foundation of my soul, I needed to be in the presence of God all the time to get through it.

The Shooting of My Oldest Son

Satan did not stop with his attempts and attacks. No

mother ever wants to receive a call that her son or child has not only been shot four times. It was mid-morning, and I was working in another county that required me to travel more than 30 miles to the main highway and another 30 minutes to the hospital where my son was being taken. I got into my car and began to pray and call on the name of Jesus. I began to speak, decree, and declare life; and to rebuke and bind death all in the name of Jesus.

I believe in the effectiveness of prayer. I know firsthand what living through a shooting does to a mind and what a bullet does to a body, and I believe that my sons' recovery and healing were a direct result of prayers. I legally ran every 4-way stop signal with my hazard signals flashing on my way to get to the main highway of 85. Then I moved directly into the HOV Lane, contacting the 911 Emergency System to inform them that I was in the HOV Lane and that I did not have an HOV Pass, but I was not going to stop if anyone tried to pull me over.

The dispatcher confirmed that my son was one of the several shootings that morning and that I could continue driving without being stopped by law enforcement. When I arrived at the hospital, an unidentified male approached me and quickly identified himself as I took a defensive stance. He showed me his badge to prove his identity as a law enforcement officer. He informed me that he recognized me and that my son was alive and well. He was aware that I was a certified and mandated law enforcement officer, and that I would be strapped and ready to act against any further acts or actions committed by those who had committed the act against my son.

What the devil intended to be evil, the Lord rejected and redirected. The devil attempted to kill my son, but God! The devil waited until my son's back was turned before unleashing a barrage of bullets, striking him four times. My son is still alive, a living and breathing testament to God's grace and mercy. What God has anointed to live cannot be killed by the devil. The devil cannot take a life he did not create. Remember, the devil cannot do anything unless he seeks God. "And the Lord said to him, hast thou considered my servant Job, that there is none like him in the earth, a simple and upright man, fearing God and avoiding sin?" (Job 1:8).

After the birth of each of my children, I gave them back to God and covered them in prayer on a daily basis. I entered the hospital and called my son's name; he opened his eyes wide enough for me to know that God had heard my prayer. My son is facing years of mental and physical recovery, as well as physical rehabilitation; I pray every day that he will be relieved of physical and mental pain, that the long-term effects of the wounds will be minimal, and that he will have the strength to endure the upcoming treatments.

I had to pray for my son's invisible wounds. He is also processing his near-death experience and wondering what his new reality will be. My son is now suffering from post-traumatic stress disorder (PTSD), anxiety, and depression. I'm now praying for him to recover from his emotional trauma.

I had to pray for financial help to cover medical bills and other expenses. The financial impact of being shot is devastating for families, especially if the person injured was the family wage earner or will be disabled for the rest of their lives. I prayed for financial assistance with hospital bills, ongoing care, materials required to function properly, and ongoing mental health treatment. But I was perplexed as to how a shooting could happen and why such a terrible thing could happen to my child; I asked God, "Why" again. It should not alarm you when the enemy appears, especially when you are disrupting and disturbing his kingdom.

I was experiencing a variety of emotions following such a traumatic event. These feelings included shock, numbness, anger, disillusionment, and others. I had trouble sleeping, concentrating, eating, or remembering even simple tasks, because my thoughts were those of my son. Over time, the caring support of family and friends helped to lessen the emotional impact and ultimately make the changes brought about by the act of violence against my son more manageable.

I had to concentrate on my strength and stick to the practices I'd discovered to provide emotional relief. I had to let myself go in prayer and in God's presence, I bowed before the Lord, humbled but hurting, angry and so much more, desiring His presence and peace for my heart, mind, and soul. For this I had to engage in healthy behaviors to enhance my ability to cope with the excessive stress. I had stopped eating and when I did eat, it was not a balanced meal; I stopped sleeping and engaging in my physical activities.

"Attend to your self-care," God said to me. While it may appear counterintuitive to put yourself first, you cannot be of service to others if you are unstable.

Keep track of all your physical health requirements, making sure to eat, sleep, exercise, and stick to your normal daily routine. God whispered in a gentle way for me to pay attention to my emotional health. I had a wide range of feelings during these difficult times; I had to remember that my other children were also experiencing emotional reactions and may need my time and patience to put their feelings and thoughts in order.

I had to concentrate on my strength base. I had to stick to my God and faith practices, which had always given me emotional relief. I had to remind myself of events and people that are meaningful' and comforting myself in the knowledge that God would see me through. "What you are going through is a sign that you are about to give birth, come out of this thing that you are in," God said to me. He told me to push through the pain, not die in childbirth, and to be mindful of my language and company while in labor, as they could cause me to abort His Promise. Remember that God had made a promise to me. Listen, it doesn't matter what you're going through or how you got pregnant, push!!! And don't die outside your promise; God has also made a promise to you.

I had to push through the pain to reach God's promise; patience is required for the process. You sometimes require the timing and season of the Lord. Everything is not a quick fix. The timing of the Word of God and receiving His Promise is all about and centered on your patience. God will try the Word that He gives you to see if you will stand on it no matter what.

When there is no answer, no way out, and no end in sight; patience is what is required to close your mouth and praise until God calls you out. While you wait, you must praise God. Don't fight the process when God is trying to set you up. *Romans 5:1 KJV: Therefore, being justified by faith, we have peace with God through our Lord Jesus Christ.*

Your suffering teaches how to patiently wait, trust, and depend on God. Patience Must Be Perfected!!! In your tribulation period-season you must have an anyhow praise. *Ecclesiastes 9:11 KJV, I returned, and saw under the sun, that the race is not to the swift, nor the battle to the strong, neither yet bread to the wise, nor yet riches to men of understanding, nor yet favour to men of skill; but time and chance happeneth to them all.*

I had to persevere and put my trust in God to get not only myself, but also, my son and his siblings through the difficult days ahead. I had to remember who I was and Whom that I was; *1st Peter 2:9; NKJV, "But you are a chosen generation, a royal priesthood, a holy nation, His own special people, to praise Him who has called you." I am chosen, a royal priesthood!*

"A royal priesthood; a holy nation, a people for God's own possession", Peter is describing a new people who will proclaim God's praise among the nations and whose priestly sacrifices will take the form of mutual submission and honoring others before themselves.

My son is recovering and doing very well, and please listen, should you ever experience such an act of violence, please seek help as needed. It is important to ask for help if you are having trouble recovering and everyday tasks seem difficult to manage.

Grandson Injured While Playing Sports

Meanwhile, my son was recovering, and I was still recovering from the experience, when I received word that my grandson, the son of my son who had been shot four times, had been injured in a football game. He was injured, not moving, and was being airlifted to a Florida hospital, according to the call. When I got the call, I was leaving the scene where my son had been shot, I pulled into the nearest parking lot and began to pray, speak, decree, and declare over my grandson's body.

God has given us the ability to speak things into existence, to declare and decree; to declare is to state a fact out loud; to "decree" is to issue a command with authority. You can have whatever you say; you always get in your life what you believe for and what you say," the Bible says you can have what you say. When you decree and declare, you have to do that using scriptural support. Since mankind is made in the image of God (Genesis 1:27), we, like God, can speak and make things happen. God spoke things into existence (Genesis 1:3, 6, 9, 14, 20, 24, 26), so those with faith can do the same.

The Apostle John said that "This is the confidence that we have in him, that if we ask anything according to His will, He hears us" (1 John 5:14). Jesus is God and He said, "Heaven and earth will pass away, but my words will not pass away" (Matt 24:35). I could not be there physically, but I had the God given power to send the word of healing to my grandson.

During the game my grandson was injured and had to be air lifted by helicopter to Gainesville Florida because of his injuries. I immediately called the hospital and was told that he had not arrived and to call back. I had previously been told that I would not be able to get any information over the phone because I was not his parent; I shared with the person I had contacted in the hospital and informed them I was his grandmother and let them know my public safety connection. She took down my contact information and promised to let me know when he arrived. I received a call that he had arrived and was being checked out for further tests. The next call that I received was that he was alert, talking, being admitted for overnight observation and that he was moving.

Isaiah 61:1, "The Spirit of the Lord GOD *is* upon me; because the LORD hath anointed me to preach good tidings unto the meek; he hath sent me to bind up the brokenhearted, to proclaim liberty to the captives, and the opening of the prison to them that are bound;"

God's mandate is the proclamation of His Word. We are all called in some way to spread the Gospel, to spread the good news, to talk to people we live with, work with, and do business with about what the Lord has done for us as we travel through life's highways and byways. The one who is sent, who is called and sent for that very purpose, the one whose business it is, whose calling it is, whose life it is to be about the business of proclaiming the good news of the Gospel to the sick. What Isaiah is saying is that God calls, sets apart, and empowers those who are called to that purpose with His Spirit. God takes the initiative, God calls, God equips, and God empowers.

What is your God given mandate? What is the mandate of the Church?

Ladies and gentlemen if all you are seeking in ministry is to be recognized by people for your gift and not for the approval of God, you are in ministry for the wrong reason. Yes, ministry will get you the titles and the papers, but it will not get the anointing of God, the power of The Holy Spirit.

To be used within any 5-fold ministry office, you first must receive a mandate from God. A mandate is an assignment placed for completion. This mandate is the "why" of your calling; it is the reason why were you called to the 5-fold ministry or office. The mandate contains the message that holds the spirit you must release to the Body of Christ to fulfill call and assignment. Receiving your mandate in addition to knowing what office you are called to is the key to the impartation you mustreceive and give to others that will come forth after you.

A "Mandate" is a formal order, assignment, or commission to do or complete something. The power granted to an elected group of people, such as a government, to carry out a specific action or govern a country: A mandated office is a 5-fold office. A mandated office requires an officer to respond to and act on a specific 5-fold mandate and commission; to act on an authoritative order or command. Moses received his mandate from God in the burning bush and was then sent by God to fulfill His commission, after which Moses became a lawgiver to God's people. Abraham, like so many others, had a mandate. Do you know you have a "mandate?

CONCLUSION

The "Call", The "Charge" and The "Mandate"

I was chosen before I was formed in my mother's womb, I had to answer the call, the call of being chosen; my invitation was in Matthew 22. There, Jesus shared a parable on "Many are called, but few are chosen"; it was a parable about an invitation to a great banquet and feast, but the guest of honor did not respond because their personal life was more important. These people were the Jews; another appeal was made to those on the streets (the Gentiles), and they responded in both good and bad ways! It is not about the call, otherwise called the invitation, but about the person.

I was fleeing an honorable invitation from the King of Kings and the Lord of Lords! I looked for God in all the wrong places and people, but everything I needed was in the Lord; do not allow anyone to pull you away from God's plan). *But He knows the path I take: when He tests me, I will come forth as gold (Job 23:10 KJV).*

When I truly accepted the call, I developed an insatiable hunger and thirst for God. There was something inside of me that would well up and cry out, something inside of me that could and would not be denied. There was and is something special about being in GOD's presence! I thought I heard Him calling to me. His voice was clear, but I had some unresolved hurts and issues that I felt I had to deal with; I wanted to deal with myself. I had no idea that all I had to do was hand it over to Him, cast it all on Him, and leave it there.

I first had to humble myself, stop running and yield to the call. God knows our beginnings and endings; He is aware of everything we intend to do, our actions, and the paths we will take. He is aware of His creations because He created everything. I misunderstood my pain and let my fleshly desires rule over me, my mind, and my life; your flesh will only destroy you! The Lord was always with me, He never left me, and He had a plan. He uses your problems to demonstrate His power to you. I had no choice but to die to my flesh as it had done me nothing but evil. My flesh overrode mind and took over my heart and the mouth speak from the heart. The flesh can be extremely dangerous and powerful!

If the devil can gain control of your mind, your thoughts, he is now in control, and you have to fight to regain that control. My mind was the devil's playground; I was roaming in the wilderness, and I did not even know it. I had to die to my Flesh and I had to get my mind right because at that point, everything about me was carnal.

My mind is where satan infiltrated and caused me to have suicidal thoughts as a teen. I had a lot to learn, but I felt like I had to learn the hard way. Accepting the call was simple, but walking the walk was a daily battle. I had to learn to live while remaining saved and under covering. I slipped and straddled the fence a few times, but greater was He that was within me, than that of the world.

You cannot serve two masters at the same time; you must submit yourself to the righteousness of God or the sinful nature of the devil. Demons are assigned to us by the devil, to cause us fall but God helps us to be aware.

Listen, you have been given permission by God to prosper. Whatever you give to God, He will multiply it. I had to relinquish control of my mind and life to The Spirit of The Living God and I had the best hookup ever; the power of my misunderstood pain had now charged me! Without God's empowerment, you can never fulfill God's plan and purpose. The charge is something that must be experienced; there is nothing I can say about the charge because everyone's experience is unique and one that you will never forget. Man can charge you, but nothing compares to the charge of GOD!

Instead of asking God why, I began to ask, "Who am I?" And it was then that I had an encounter with the "I AM". I didn't have an identity crisis anymore; well, I've never had an identity crisis because I used to let others tell me who I was. I did not desire the call that had been set into stone but there was something on the inside that could and would not be denied.

I recognized, realized, and accepted the truth in the words of JoAnne Marshall Brunson, Mother Corine Manuel, and Apostle Bettye White. These women of God had an ear to hear God's voice and the boldness to obey and speak His Words, His Truth. The truth of my being in the pit, but that God had predestined me for the Place in The Kingdom of GOD; He will redeem the time.

Every word spoken by the women in my childhood, adolescence, young adulthood, and adulthood was confirmed by Mother Prophetess Corine Manuel, Apostle Betty White, Apostle Vanessia M. Livingston, Mother Estella Boyd, Dr. Gertrude Stacks, Minister Jerolene Wilburn, Bishop Dianne R. Collins, Mother Judy Hines, Mother Dorothy Boyd Rush, and Many Others. Everything that came out of me was part of God's plan for my life—for me. Whatever you are going through is only a prelude to what God will do in your life.

You must understand what the Lord is looking for and what the devil is after. You must be reborn; remove all hurt and pain from your memory; get everything out of your ear; get around people who cause you to change. Prepare to work.

I am grateful to GOD for Kingdom Mothers and connections, great people with great minds and visions.

You need people who have GOD in them to speak into and over your life. You must understand the "Power of Agreement"; do not agree with people who will agree with everything you do but will call you out when you need it; people who will check you and you will not have an attitude. Yes, you may be an adult, but you need a checker, someone who can see the outcome and expectation of GOD over your life. I thank GOD for my checkers and spiritual coverings. I say a big thank you to you all for your presence and for allowing me to sit at your Feet as you poured into me to bring the outcome of GOD'S expectations over my life.

I made a vow to the Lord that if He would get me out of whatever was holding me back, that stronghold, I would go where He said to go, do what He said to do, and say what He said to say. He answered me and said, "If you walk upright, live holy, and speak My words; not a word that you shall speak will hit the ground or return to you void."

As I wrap this up, please allow me to leave you with a few nuggets to know and remember.

- A strong prayer life is mandatory, and a must. Pray and get into the very presence of GOD.
- It takes prayer to have an anointing and no prayer hinders the move of GOD in your life.
- Prayer produces power to perform GOD'S purpose and plan for your life.
- Your first ministry is prayer.
- Stop settling for church relationship or membership and become kingdom minded. Rid yourself of the form of Godliness.
- Remember your words have power.
- Know then that labor amongst you.
- Get around people that will make you change.
- God will not use anyone that is not yielded or anyone not in a covenant with Him. You must yield your mind, body and spirit.
- Get everything out of your ear, but God.
- A Christian life is a lifestyle and a lifetime of sacrifices.
- God put me in it and through it to get the victory as a Job/Jobette.
- Victory belongs to Jesus always.
- Your outcome will not change until you change your mind; the way you think.
- You must labor.
- Never lose faith.

- There is always a tribulation period/season, and sometimes you have to deal with embarrassments and humiliation of God telling you something and the outcome was not what you expected.
- There is a set time and season in your life when the enemy cannot do anything with it and this will be the time when GOD says, "I am going to bring order to your chaos."
- Whatever you are going through, do not allow it to stress you, God is still on the throne; praise Him until things shift.
- Whatever it is no matter what, put prayer and praise on it.
- Pray until doors open, chains are destroyed and fall off, turn around happens, deliverance comes, healing takes place.
- Pray until the fire falls.
- Do not allow your wombs to become old and deep.
- You must release the hurt, the pain and the remembrance of it all. Let it go!!!
- You must know and recognize demons and demonic spirits.
- We have the power and authority over the devil and all evil.
- Never become a slave to your sins.
- Never die spiritually.
- Use your power and authority to command things to happen.
- When God speaks, He makes it clear and you understand.
- Thank the Lord GOD Always.

Every Prophecy Spoken to Me, Over My Life and Ministry, Has Been Held and Remains Kept Within My Heart So That I May Draw from Them for Guidance and Strength; for These

Words Were the Lord's Concerning Me, My Life, and Prophetess Dr. Marie Baker's Ministry. But I had to Hear, to Obey, to Totally Commit/ Humbly Submit" to Christ and Go Through The Ranks of The Process (There Is a Process) of Development and Grooming.

That Process Consists of a Series of Actions or Steps That Must Be Completed in Order to Achieve a Specific End-Goal. God Has Orchestrated and Designated People, Places, Tests, and Trials to Make Things Happen, and Help You Shift to The Next level of Your Purpose and Promise.

If I Knew What I Know Now, I Would Have Said Yes Sooner Than I Did. Again, I Am So Glad That I Made the Choice to Walk Away from My Sins of Being a Queen Pin; I was Transformed from "Queendom to Kingdom"; from the Pit to the Palace. I Now Am "His Queen in His Kingdom", "Gods Kingdom".

I Made an Investment into Myself by "Waiting On and in God".I Am "Healthy", "Happy" and "Wealthy" In God.

Luke 12:32 KJV says, "Fear Not, Little Flock; For It Is Your Father's Good Pleasure to Give You The "Kingdom." Lord, I Thank You for My Life in Your Kingdom.

I Hope and Pray that This Book Has Encouraged, Enlightened and Inspired Your Life and Walk in Christ.

My Prayer for You Is That Heaven Smiles Upon You and GOD Richly Bless You.

ABOUT DR. MARIE BAKER

*Prophetess Dr. Marie Baker AA, BA, BS, MA, M Div. Ph.D.

*Honorary Doctorate in Humanitarianism

*Presidential Lifetime Achievement Award

Authors Contact Information:

PMB Ministries International Judah Dove LLC
Kingdom Come Atlanta LLC 3628 Satellite Blvd #958196
Duluth Ga, 30095
Phone 706-386-4698 / 678-628-7960
Email: QueenBBaker@gmail.Com
PMBMinistries@gmail.com
Website: JudahDove.Org

Made in the USA
Columbia, SC
01 October 2024